Encounters with the Living Christ

Meeting Jesus in the Gospel of John

Robert B. Setzer Jr.

Judson Press
Valley Forge

Encounters with the Living Christ: Meeting Jesus in the Gospel of John
© 1999 by Judson Press, Valley Forge, PA 19482-0851

All rights reserved.

Bible quotations in this volume, unless otherwise indicated, are from the New Revised Standard Version of the Bible, copyright © 1989 by the Division of Christian Education of the National Council of the Churches of Christ in the United States of America. Used by permission. All rights reserved. Bible quotations marked KJV are from The Holy Bible, King James Version. Bible quotations marked NIV are from the HOLY BIBLE: New International Version, copyright © 1973, 1978, 1984. Used by per-mission of Zondervan Bible Publishers. Bible quotations marked THE JERUSALEM BIBLE are from The Jerusalem Bible, Copyright © 1966 by Darton, Longman & Todd, Ltd. and Doubleday and Company, Inc. Used by permission of the publisher. Bible quotations marked TLB are from The Living Bible, copyright © 1971. Used by permission of Tyndale House Publishers, Inc., Wheaton, IL 60189. All rights reserved. Italicized typeface in Bible quotations indicate author's emphasis.

Library of Congress Cataloging-in-Publication Data

Setzer, Robert B.
Encounters with the living Christ: meeting Jesus in the Gospel of John/ Robert B. Setzer, Jr.
    p. cm.
    ISBN 0-8170-1288-5 (pbk.: alk. paper)
    1. Bible. N.T. John—Criticism, interpretation, etc. 2. Jesus Christ—Person and offices—Biblical teaching. 3. Christian life—Biblical teaching.
I. Title.
BS2615.2.S466 1999
226.5'06—dc21   98-44189

Printed in the U.S.A.
06 05 04 03 02 01 00 99
10 9 8 7 6 5 4 3 2 1

To Mom, for teaching me the Story.
To Dad, for living it.
In them, for me, the Word first became flesh.
And that
made all the difference.

Contents

Foreword

Marcus Borg recently wrote a best-selling book entitled *Meeting Jesus Again for the First Time*. Borg's encounter with Jesus came primarily as a result of his study of the synoptic gospels, Matthew, Mark, and Luke. In this volume Bob Setzer speaks of his experience of "Meeting Jesus Again for the Second Time," but he specifically considers the role John's Gospel played in that encounter.

Setzer, like all passionate writers, has a case to make. Having been hooked on John's Gospel himself, he is out to get you to read thoughtfully, imaginatively, and redemptively the Fourth Gospel. I'll bet that is precisely the way John wanted you to read his Gospel—thoughtfully, imaginatively, and redemptively. Setzer's gratitude for the Fourth Gospel simply cannot be suppressed. He has written his book because he wants you to read John's book. To read this book, says Setzer, without reading John's book is like reading about astronomy and never "peering into a star-studded night" (p. 10).

But one thing is even more important to Setzer than the Gospel of John, and that is the portrait of the Christ that John paints. The faithful pastoral evangelist that he is, Setzer longs for you to meet the Living Christ of John's Gospel. He wants you to fall for John's Gospel, hoping that you will end up where Thomas did—at the feet of Christ, saying, "My Lord and my God!" Setzer works from the assumption that "the enduring power" of John's Gospel is that it was "written in the conviction that Jesus Christ can be as real in our lives today as he was for those who first knew and loved him" (p. xx).

Writing with that conviction, Setzer's own descriptive language brings the events of John's Gospel to life. His description of Jesus "cleansing the temple" takes you to the scene live and in living color:

classes, and theological discussion groups will find it an especially helpful guide to John's Gospel. The questions at the end
of the chapters are uniquely suggestive. Often study questions
at the end of book chapters are feeble efforts at making the
book more marketable. Setzer's questions at the end of his
chapters are provocative, text-related questions that cause one
to understand the Gospel of John better while relating it to the
struggles of contemporary life. But if you are like me, you will
also find yourself reading Setzer's questions and wondering,
"How would the folks in 'Adults, Too, Sunday school' or
'Koheleth' or 'Parchment Club' answer some of these?" In other
words, for a group to address these questions together would
facilitate a better understanding not only of the Gospel of John
but of one another.

Additionally, this is an excellent book for personal study.
When I read this manuscript, I sought to do what Bob Setzer
asked of the reader. I read again John's Gospel as I read Setzer's
chapters. It was a spiritually rewarding exercise. Try it.

Walter B. Shurden
Callaway Professor of Christianity
Chair, Department of Christianity
Mercer University, Macon, Georgia

Introduction

It was the first Bible I remember.

A colorful cover showing Jesus with a circle of children huddled around him invited young readers inside. I wanted to meet that wonderful man who had a soft spot in his heart for little people like me.

Of course, the first two-thirds of the Book was pretty foreboding territory—a lot of "begats" and long names and strange stories. It was difficult reading for a nine-year-old, so I trusted my mom and Sunday school teachers to hit the high spots.

But in my longing to meet the man on the cover, I knew enough to turn to the Gospels: Matthew, Mark, Luke, and John. That was where the story of Jesus was told in all of its wonder and glory. So whenever I opened my brightly covered children's Bible, I usually went to the opening books of the New Testament. There the words of Jesus were printed in red, so I knew when he was speaking. Often when reading I felt as if he were speaking directly to me.

That was especially true when reading the Gospel of John. There those red words of Jesus glowed with white-hot intensity. Matthew, Mark, and Luke were all a good read, but the Jesus in them kept his distance. In John's Gospel he got up close and personal. It was as though he drew near when I read, looking over my shoulder, whispering the words. And so it went for several years: John's Gospel was hallowed ground where I could go and meet with Jesus.

But with the passing of the years, I grew up and became a little more sophisticated. With a college Bible course or two under my belt, I learned that maybe Jesus didn't speak every word attributed to him in John's Gospel. After all, John's Jesus made stunning claims completely missing in the other three Gospels: "The Father and I are *one*" (John 10:30), for instance.

And material crucial in other Gospels was not included: the Sermon on the Mount and the parables being two notable examples.[1] Further, some of John's most memorable and important scenes were missing in Matthew, Mark, and Luke: the encounter with the woman at the well (chap. 4) and the raising of Lazarus (chap. 11) to name but two.

As I began to read John's Gospel with a more skeptical eye, those words printed in red began to fade. And they didn't just fade to black. Eventually they faded altogether from view as I came to distrust John's portrayal of Jesus, never sure what was fact and what was fiction.

And with the fading of those words in red came a fading of Jesus' presence. He came to be more and more an enigmatic figure from the past and less and less an unseen companion in the joys and struggles of daily life.

I then set about trying to find the "real Jesus." Armed with the best of scholarly tools, I started pecking away at what I had come to believe were crusty layers of pious tradition. Like an archaeologist on a dig, I approached the New Testament—and especially the Gospels—as once sacred ground where some ancient treasures were buried. If only I could scrape away all the elaborations and exaggerations of the writers, I might discover who Jesus really was. And with a little luck—or even providence—some frayed fragment of my once vital childhood faith might remain intact.

My quest for the historical Jesus, however, was unsuccessful, for I found that the Jesus who emerged from my archaeological expeditions looked too much like me. Little wonder since consciously and unconsciously I tended to reject as inauthentic any material that didn't fit my preconceived notion of him: an insightful teacher and rabbi, no doubt. But if the historical Jesus ever really said, "The Father and I are one," he was surely a megalomaniac rather than *a* son—much less *the Son*— of God.

---

[1] To these could be added the story of Jesus' birth, the temptations in the wilderness, the confession at Caesarea-Philippi, the Transfiguration, the exorcisms, and more besides.

Thus, from my exalted pinnacle of supposed detached and objective enlightenment, I dissected and dismissed the witness of the Gospels at will. Mostly blind to the arrogance fueling my efforts, I became smug and self-satisfied. And in the process, instead of finding Jesus, I lost him. I lost him beneath a huge mound of unanswered questions, qualifications, and quibbles.

But by some miracle of grace, Jesus never lost me. He continued to haunt my dreams and to tease my waking moments from just off-stage of full awareness. He surprised me in strange coincidences that smacked of his touch. He shone in the faces of ordinary believers who had not lost sight of him. But mostly he called to me not so much from his presence, as from the deepening ache of his absence.

At last, weary and worn, I turned once more to John in search of Jesus. But I came to his witness this time not as a naive child, but as a battered, cynical, beat-up adult. I came as a homeless man approaches a soup kitchen: angry at being reduced to such a public confession of his need but desperate for food. And so I opened this Gospel once more, not really expecting much, but needing and wanting more than I dared put into words.

There was no magic, at least not at first—no earthshaking revelations, no radical reversals, no instantaneous transformations—just a growing awareness that in the darkness of my doubt and disbelief the hint of dawn was beginning to shine. I continued to quarrel with John and accuse him of stretching the facts. But I could also hear in the pages of his witness the hint of laughter, as if just over my shoulder someone was enjoying a chuckle at my expense, amused that I feared John was saying too much for Jesus when the real irony was that for all of John's exalted poetry and prose he couldn't tell the half.

Reading on for some weeks and months, the faint light of dawn glowed brighter. I became enamored with the possibility of "what if?" What if Jesus really was—really is—who John declared him to be? Just the thought of that put goose bumps on my heart. And sometimes the dawn light seemed pregnant with a figure of radiance and beauty about to step over the horizon. But deeply invested in a view of myself as poised and in control, I refused to allow my childlike awe and wonder to scream, "Look! It's Jesus!"

At last, in an early morning rendezvous with John's Gospel, I could contain the confession no longer. The light of dawn flared up bright and a great ball of illumination appeared on the horizon. Instinctively I bowed my head and shut my eyes. But the stinging light would not be denied, and the darkness of my inner world shimmered with glory.

Then the light receded, and a very human Jesus remained. He looked like the figure on the cover of my childhood Bible. Sitting on a rock, he beckoned me near. Gingerly I approached, painfully aware of my betrayals and defections. But eyes full of love encouraged me on until at last, with great strong arms, he pulled me onto his lap. Huddled there, the shame of forsaking him proved overwhelming. My shoulders began to heave, and out came a great torrent of tears.

As I wept adult-sized pain through a child's unabashed tears, Jesus pulled me close. "I've missed you, Bobby," he said. "It's been a long time." I buried my head in his shoulder, sobbing harder still.

But those tears were the birth waters of a new beginning. And for the second time in my life, I was reborn.

It was something of a shock to discover upon returning to John's Gospel with newly opened eyes, that John never claimed to be providing a verbatim report of Jesus' words and deeds in the first place. And neither did the other Gospel writers for that matter. In fact, they created an entirely new literary vehicle for conveying their world-altering encounter with Jesus Christ: a confessional history called a Gospel. These Gospels were not—are not—mythology, meaning abstract truths given narrative expression. After all, the conviction that in Jesus Christ, the "Word became flesh" (John 1:14)—a real, flesh and blood person from first-century Nazareth—is the cornerstone of John's witness.

On the other hand, the Gospels do not claim to be unbiased, documentary history. That kind of language wasn't even invented until after the Enlightenment. No, the Gospels are carefully crafted confessions of who Jesus is as seen in the light of Easter. For it was the riveting realization that Jesus had triumphed over sin and death that birthed the Church. It was the appearance of the risen Christ, radiant with glory and life, that led his followers to fathom fully who he was and is. Naturally, they were driven to reevaluate his life and ministry in light of that world-shattering event.

There is no pretending otherwise in John's Gospel, for he tells us directly. In recounting the cleansing of the temple (2:13-22), John reports Jesus' shocking statement, "Destroy this temple and in three days, I will raise it up" (v. 19). Clearly those present were startled by the saying. John even steps in to offer a helpful footnote to the reader: "He was speaking of the temple of his body." Then he goes on to add, "After he was raised from the dead, his disciples remembered that he had said this; and they believed the scripture and the word that Jesus had spoken" (2:22).

So it was that in the light of Easter, many of the words and deeds of Jesus' life—terribly unnerving and puzzling at the time—took on new meaning. Or better said, their original intent and meaning were clearly revealed.

I remember a time when a friend of mine acted uncharacteristically rude. Her behavior left me puzzled and miffed. Later I discovered the offense had occurred shortly after she learned she had a malignant tumor. Suddenly I understood. Her behavior—strange at the time—made perfect sense in light of that revelation.

In an infinitely greater way, the meaning of Jesus' life and the depths of his person could not be fully apprehended until Easter. But after his death and resurrection the missing pieces to the puzzle started falling into place. His followers looked back on a particular event in light of Easter, and suddenly, insight crystallized and realization dawned: "So *that* is what he meant!"

Again, John shows us the hand he is playing. In John's Gospel, Jesus says, "I still have many things to say to you, but you cannot bear them now. When the Spirit of truth comes, he will guide you into all the truth; for he will not speak on his own, but will speak whatever he hears, and he will declare to you the things that are to come" (16:12-13). In other words, there were many things Jesus wished to tell his disciples that they simply could not fathom. But in the light of Jesus' Easter rising, they received the gift of the Holy Spirit (20:22) and began to understand.

Thus, for the believing community—whether in John's day or our own—the critical question is not, Did the historical Jesus make such and such a statement or do such and such a thing? Rather, the critical question is this: Does John's witness provide a clear and compelling witness to *who Jesus is?* That is a terribly important question each person must answer for himself or herself. I am building a life on the conviction that John's portrait of Jesus, while doubtless impressionistic in style, renders a real and vivid likeness of the Master.

Again, this does not mean John was free to *invent* material, as though he were writing a collection of religious short stories. The conviction permeating his Gospel—that in Jesus Christ the eternal Son of God took a face within time—is the ground of the Christian's assurance that both our history and our humanity matter to God. The writer of the Fourth Gospel purports to be an eyewitness to the events of Jesus' life, and there is every evidence he was: "He who saw this has testified so that you also may believe. His testimony is true, and he knows that he tells the truth" (19:35).[2]

On the other hand, the author of the Fourth Gospel did feel free to *interpret* the events of Jesus' life in light of Easter. Indeed, to do anything less would have been to misrepresent the decisive significance of God's self-disclosure in Jesus Christ. That's why in everything the author wrote he was guided by this charter: "Now Jesus did many other signs in the presence of his disciples, which are not written in this book. But these are written so you may come to believe that Jesus is the Messiah, the Son of God, and that through believing you may have life in his name" (20:30-31).

---

2 For other references to the author, see 13:23; 19:26; 20:2-10; 21:7, 20, 24.

The Author and Unique Character of the Fourth Gospel

Who was the author of the Fourth Gospel? The title— "The Gospel According to John"—was added later as this Gospel began to circulate among the churches. The title reflects the consensus of the early Church that this work goes back to John, the son of Zebedee, one of Jesus' twelve disciples. The author describes himself simply as the "disciple Jesus loved" and is remembered as the "beloved disciple."[3] It may be that this author's original witness was expanded somewhat by others who knew him and wrote in his wake.[4] But that is conjecture; we can't know for certain. We only know that early on, this Gospel—along with the other three—was recognized as providing an authentic witness to the life and enduring significance of Jesus. That is why the four Gospels were canonized and made the foundation of the Christian New Testament.

Around 200 C.E. the early Church father Clement of Alexandria made a revealing observation about the Gospel of John: "John, last of all, conscious that the outward facts had been set forth in the Gospels, was urged on by his disciples, and, divinely moved by the Spirit, composed a spiritual Gospel."[5] That is an apt way to describe the difference in feeling and tone between John and the first three Gospels: John is more "spiritual," more given to symbolism and metaphor, more inclined to peek behind the curtain and tell us what is going on backstage. But this does not mean that his Gospel is "less true" than the other three; in fact, as judged by John's use of the word "true"—meaning, revelatory of God's saving presence in Jesus Christ—his Gospel may be truest of all.[6]

---

3 See note 2 above.

4 Commonly called the "Johannine School," evidence of such further editing is found in the "we passages" of the Fourth Gospel (cf. 3:11a; 21:24). The Johannine School is also thought to have composed 1, 2, and 3 John and the Revelation.

5 As quoted by Eusebius, writing around AD 30. Quoted in Larry Kreizer, *Regent's Study Guides 1: The Gospel According to John* (Oxford: Regent's Park College, 1990), 5.

6 Cf. 1:17; 8:32.

In reading this Gospel, don't trouble yourself trying to decide what comes from the mouth of the historical Jesus and what comes from the risen Christ speaking through the power of the Holy Spirit. The truth is, the scholarly consensus on such matters rises and falls like the stock market. One must check frequently to see what the current valuation of a given word or deed of Jesus happens to be.

But for John, the words and works of the historical Jesus— and the risen Christ speaking through the words of this Gospel—are all of a piece. For it is the *same Lord Jesus* in either event, drawing near in the presence of his Spirit today as surely as he drew near to those first disciples while among them in the flesh. Only now the living Christ, robed in his Easter glory, communes with his disciples in the power of his Word and Spirit and in the life of his people, the Church.

That's the enduring power of this Gospel. It was written in the conviction that Jesus Christ can be as real in our lives today as he was for those who first knew and loved him. If you are not a Christian, you may find that hard to believe. And even if you are a Christian but have lost your way, you may wistfully remember a faith you believe is lost forever.

That need not be. You can encounter the living Christ— even today. Or better said, you can be awakened to the realization that he is waiting to encounter you. But first one must pry open a cynical, cold heart and let the light of his risen presence call forth new life.

Just one word of caution: Don't play around with this Gospel. It is full of explosive material. These words have ignited the fire of a living faith in Jesus Christ in many a burned-out skeptic like myself. Reading this Gospel with an open mind and eager heart just might change your life.

Take it from someone who knows.

Good Friday, 1998
Bob Setzer Jr.

CHAPTER 1

The Human Face of Holy Love

John 1:1-18

SEVENTEEN, a freshman in college. "On the rebound," as they say, he was not looking for any romantic involvements. The plan was to date around and focus on securing his position as a big man on campus.

Then walking across campus one brisk fall day, he saw a brown-eyed beauty drawing near. Her dark tan, demure smile, and graceful spirit immediately stirred his interest. Instinctively, he was drawn to her, so he cockily strode up to make her acquaintance. As introductions and greetings were exchanged, he felt himself slipping over the edge of some unseen precipice. Those big, brown eyes, sparkling with laughter and life, bid him near. Then she blinked, and like the mighty Goliath felled by a tiny stone from David's sling, he fell for her. And he fell hard.

Quite without intending it, he found himself transfixed by this lovely young woman. But still reeling from love lost, he was skittish about commitment. So for weeks to come, he and the pretty coed teased and flirted but never touched. Still, his love for her was growing. But like a bulb germinating beneath the surface of the earth, no one could see.

Finally, he could contain the love no longer. Some wild impulse led him to put words to music. And from his heart of hearts the hidden love erupted into view. "I love you," he said, his face flushed with both fear and longing.

Her eyes shimmered, then glistened. "I love you too," she said. Their lips met to form a kiss. A word of love became flesh.

And a communion of hearts once only potential became concrete and real.

Twenty years later the love sealed by that kiss still holds.
I should know, for I was the boy with the love that became a
word, a kiss, a marriage, a life.

God also had a word to share. From the very beginning it
was a word lodged deep within God's heart: "In the beginning
was the Word, and the Word was with God, and the Word was
God" (John 1:1). Never was there a time when that word was
not woven into the very essence of the divine Being.

Then God dared to speak the divine Word of love (1:3).
Into the darkness that reigned before creation's dawn, the living
God cried, "'Let there be light'; and there *was* light" (Genesis
1:3). Living and powerful and sharper than any two-edged
sword (Hebrews 4:12), the God-Word split the primeval chaos
into order.[1] And from the order God called forth life. And from
the miracle of life God called forth a unique, living embodiment
of divine love: a man and woman crafted in God's own image
(Genesis 1:27). Breathing the very breath of God (Genesis 2:7),
the twosome reveled in the divine presence and played and
danced by angel light.

Then something went terribly wrong. The man and woman
turned against God, themselves, and each other (Genesis 3:1-
7). Soon they were perishing in a self-imposed exile of their
own shame. Even God's Word of love sounded shrill to their
ears, so they covered their ears and huddled in the darkness
(Genesis 3:8) until at last God found them and confronted them
with their betrayal of holy love. Then a merciful Lord covered
the wayward children with animal skins so that they could
bear to face each other (Genesis 3:21). And then, brokenhearted
and weeping, the Lord God of all creation banished them from
the divine presence (Genesis 3:23-24).

In the millennia that followed, an ever-gracious God continued speaking the word of love. God reached out to a chosen
people through mighty acts of deliverance and the words of

---

[1] The "God-Word" is my adaptation of Robert Kysar's term, the "Christ-Word."
See Robert Kysar, *John's Story of Jesus*. (Philadelphia: Fortress Press, 1984), 15.

God's prophets. But the human creatures, yet mired in selfishness and sin, had lost their ear for God. Thus, while God's Word continued to sound, it could be perceived but faintly, as though being heard underwater. Communication was often garbled and sometimes tragically misunderstood, until many came to perceive the living God as a mortal enemy and not as the loving, attentive Parent who had birthed them and held them precious.

Finally, the living God was desperate to speak the word of love that no one could hear. So, God reached deep into the divine heart of hearts and pulled forth the Word of love present from the beginning (John 1:18). Then God melded that glorious Word into the humanity of one Jesus of Nazareth: "And the Word became flesh and lived among us" (1:14).

So it was that God's love erupted into view in a Word that became a life. And that life, lived within a flesh-and-blood person radiant with a glory divine, shattered the world's darkness (1:5). It unstopped people's ears and opened their eyes. For they saw in Jesus Christ the life and love of God drawing near. And those who *believed*—who entrusted themselves to the Holy Love now taking a human face—were awakened to their true destiny as sons and daughters of God (1:12). God's word of love, no longer merely spoken but *embodied*, brought forth a new creation.

Of course, God is not a bungling college freshman trying to speak—and embody—a hidden word of love. But in speaking of God, we are reduced to such analogies, flawed and inadequate though they be. For we can only speak of the unknown in terms that belong to the world of our own experience.

John was also drawing on the language and ideas of his time when he tried to put into words the stirring confession, "And the Word became flesh and lived among us" (1:14). In calling Jesus "the Word," he was using an expression steeped in religious and philosophical tradition.

In the cultured circles of the first century, "the Word"—or *logos* in the Greek—was a fixture of Greek literature and philosophy. It was believed the Logos represented the cosmic reason that brought meaning and order to the world.

In Jewish tradition, the concept of the "Word of God" had a long and storied history. The world was created by the Word of God (Genesis 1:3ff.), a word that continued to sound in Israel's great figures and prophets.[2] And late in the formation of the Old Testament, the Word of God even came to be personified as Wisdom.[3]

But in chapter 1 of John's Gospel, the author goes far beyond either Greek or Jewish precedents in using the "logos." First, he assigns the figure of the Logos not merely a poetic status, but a real one. Paradoxically, the Logos was both in God—"*was* God"—and yet somehow distinct—"*with* God" (v. 1). Unlike our words that have no existence apart from ourselves, John's Logos is a "he" (v. 2). Clearly, John is pushing the envelope of his cultural heritage. For him, God is not a flat, one-dimensional being, but a mysterious communion of love in which God and the God-Word are united in God the Spirit.[4]

Thus, when John writes that the "Word became flesh" (1:14), he is not talking about some abstract message or moral. Rather, he is making the dizzying claim that God's inner essence was enfleshed in a first-century Jewish carpenter from Nazareth. Unlike every other religious luminary, ancient and modern, Jesus was no mere witness to the Light (1:6-8); he *was* the Light of eternity spilling into time (1:5). He was not merely *divine* as an enchanting sunset is "divine"—reflecting the divine glory. He was the very life and love of God disclosed in a human life. Or as John says it, "We have seen *his* glory, the glory as of a father's only son, full of grace and truth" (1:14).[5]

---

2 Numbers 3:16 is typical of innumerable Old Testament texts that could be cited: "So Moses enrolled them according to the Word of the LORD, as he was commanded."

3 See, e.g., Proverbs 8:22-31.

4 Language such as this pushed the Church to formulate its notion of God as a rich tri-unity of love: God the Father, God the Son, and God the Holy Spirit. This theme will be explored more fully in chapters 8 and 13 of this book.

5 John begins his Gospel by seizing upon a word already in circulation—the "*logos.*" But here he introduces his preferred language for the relationship between Jesus and God—that of Father and Son. The Father/Son image will guide the balance of his Gospel.

And second, beyond asserting a real versus a merely symbolic status for the God-Word, John makes another equally stunning claim: he declares that this Word fully plumbed the depths of human experience: "The Word became flesh and lived among us."

Even in English, the shock of the phrase lands like a splash of cold water on the face: "The Word *became flesh!*" God's eternal, creative, all-powerful Word clothed not in angelic splendor, but in frail, pitiful flesh! But in Greek, the original language of the New Testament, the noise of alien words colliding is louder still: "The *Logos* became *sarx.*" *Sarx* is a bitter, biting word[6] because for the Greeks, the flesh was but a contaminated holding tank for the eternal spirit. It was a place one lived as one lives in a ghetto, hoping against hope one day to get out.

But John doesn't say the Word *abided* in the flesh, as a fly-by-night operator might spend a few nights in a shabby hotel. Nor does he say the Word *used* the flesh as a brilliant artist might use a canvas to render her vision. No, he goes for broke. He says the Word *became* flesh, meaning that in Jesus Christ, God so fully identified with our humanity that forever more, God knows the human situation from the inside out.

Thus, Jesus is not only God's eternal, creative, all-powerful *WORD* made flesh; he is also the Word made *FLESH*. And who's to say which is the greater miracle?

Robert Louis Stevenson delighted in the story of a ship tossed at sea. The waves were high and the rocky coast perilous and close. Knowing the danger, a sense of dread and foreboding seized the crew. One frantic sailor, laboring in the bowels of the ship, could contain himself no longer. He rushed to the control room and stood frozen in fright, watching the captain wrestle with the wheel of the great ship.

Fearless at the helm, the captain brought all his skill and strength to bear on the task of guiding the vessel through the rocky shoals into the safety of open water. Turning slightly, he noticed the frightened sailor at his side. Seeing the terror etched in the young man's face, the captain smiled at him, nodding his reassurance.

---

[6] It is the root of our word *sarcasm.*

At that, the youth returned below deck and assured the crew that all was well. When his shipmates demanded to know the source of such confidence, the sailor answered, "I have seen the face of the captain, and he smiled at me."[7]

Christians believe that in Jesus Christ they have seen the very face of the Captain—and he has smiled at us. The One at the helm of both time and eternity is not a tyrant to be feared, but a great and mighty Lord whose face is turned toward us in love and longing. For in Jesus Christ, God's holy love has taken a human face. And it is not a face contorted in anger, but radiant with grace. As the apostle Paul confesses, "It is the God who said, 'Let light shine out of darkness,' who has shone in our hearts to give the light of the . . . glory of God in the face of Jesus Christ" (2 Corinthians 4:6). Or as John exults, "No one has ever seen God. It is God the only Son, who is close to the Father's heart, who has made him known" (1:18).

And yet there is more. For the wonder of the Christian gospel is not merely that God stands over us with the answers, but that in Jesus Christ, God has *lived our questions.* For in becoming flesh, the God-Word didn't merely toy with our humanity, but entered fully into its ambiguities and struggles.

Even so, in Jesus Christ we see the eternal Son of God weeping salty tears before the grave of his beloved friend Lazarus (John 11). And we see him lashing out in anger at the money changers in the temple (John 2). We see him stooped and beaten before a well, desperate for a drink (John 4). We see him struggling to be faithful to his calling as the looming spectacle of the cross drew near: "Now my soul is troubled. And what should I say—'Father, save me from this hour'?" (John 12:27).

Even in John's Gospel—which emphasizes Jesus' *God*hood more than his *man*hood—there can be no doubting: in this carpenter turned rabbi turned Savior, we see a real flesh-and-blood person taking history's stage. And instinctively we know: he understands. He knows our heartaches, our struggles, and our weaknesses. There is no facet of our experience utterly foreign

---

7 *Parables, etc.* 8, no. 7 (July 1988), 2.

to him. And thus is formed the Christian's grand confidence: because of Jesus Christ, God knows our hearts.[8]

In a *New York Times Magazine* essay entitled "Alone in a Lofty Place," Barbara Grizzuti Harrison writes about her conversion from being a Jehovah's Witness to a devout Catholic. Central to this radical shift was her emerging conviction that, in Jesus Christ, God fully plumbed the depths of human experience.

> The Witnesses insisted that Jesus was merely a Son of God, not God Himself; but how very much less desirable and attractive He is if He is only Daddy's brave best boy, prophet, social worker, revolutionary. It is because God suffered in His flesh and soul the torments and anguish of human life that we, broken and askew, are able to cast ourselves upon him.[9]

Yes, it is a stunning, revolutionary pronouncement: that in Jesus Christ, the God-Word—present *in* and *with* God from the beginning—indwelt and hallowed a human life. Indeed, it would have been unthinkable apart from the staggering impact Jesus Christ had on those who knew and loved him. But when they looked into his face, they saw a light that shone brighter than all the constellations of the night. And in his eyes, shimmering with holy fire, they caught glimpses of God.

Others may wish to reduce the gospel to certain timeless truths, but John knew better. He knew that what was timeless about the gospel was not Jesus' teaching—revolutionary though it was—but Jesus himself. For the gospel was and is the story of God entering the human fray not in words, but in person. And in the face and touch and embrace of the Master, God's love began to heal and transform a broken world.

---

[8] As the writer of Hebrews says it, "For we do not have a high priest who is unable to sympathize with our weaknesses, but we have one who in every respect has been tested as we are, yet without sin" (4:15).

[9] *The New York Times Magazine*, December 7, 1997, 73.

Granted, that's a lot to swallow. From the beginning, many choked on the confession. Not everyone believed God was uniquely and decisively present in Jesus: "He came unto his own, and his own received him not" (1:11, KJV).

But to all who believed—to all who took a wild and daring chance on Jesus—he gave power to become sons and daughters of God (1:12). And they discovered in their own experience that God was not a despot to be feared, but a doting heavenly Father to be treasured and adored.

Is it possible for people yet today to have that joyous confidence in their hearts? Yes, it is possible. For John left this Gospel like a handkerchief dropped in the woods marking the spot where lovers meet. He left it so you could find what he found, namely, the light and love of God shining in the face of the Nazarene.[10]

Up for a dare? Read John's witness with an eager, attentive heart. Ponder his words with the throttle of your imagination wide open. Ask God to speak to your deepest need and highest aspiration. Just for a little spell, bracket your cynicism and let this Gospel work its magic. See if the light that shattered the darkness in the long-ago and far-away begins to shine in you. For every time the living Christ draws near, God's heartfelt word of love begins to sound in the soul.

God of grace and God of glory, we thank you
for the unspeakable gift of Jesus Christ.
Because of him, we can know you,
even as you know the depths of our humanity.
Awaken us to his living presence that we can hear
your word of love sounding deep within.
In the name of your Word made flesh,
even Jesus Christ our Lord, we pray.
Amen.

---

[10] In the final pages of his Gospel, John states this explicitly: "These [things] are written so that you may come to believe that Jesus is the Messiah, the Son of God, and that through believing you may have life in his name" (20:31).

Questions for Reflection

1. This chapter likens the *logos* to a word of love first felt, then spoken and embodied in Jesus of Nazareth. It also suggests that Jesus is the "face of the Captain" smiling at us. Can you suggest other analogies or images that reflect the oneness—yet the distinction—of Jesus and God?
2. It is commonly said of world religions, "All roads lead to the top of the mountain." In what ways does John's opening chapter challenge this notion? What to him is absolutely unique about Jesus?
3. John makes a case for the full divinity (1:1) and the full humanity (1:14) of Jesus. Most Christians emphasize one or the other of these poles. What kind of faith results when Jesus' humanity is minimized? His divinity?
4. Augustine, an early Church father, was widely read in Greek philosophy. He said he found everything he needed in Plato and Aristotle save this: "The Word became flesh and lived among us." What did that affirmation provide that philosophy alone could not?
5. In what ways does Jesus embody a convergence of "grace and truth" (1:14,17)? What does this suggest about the kind of people his followers are to be?

Trailmarker

John 1:19–12:50

This book is not a verse-by-verse commentary of the Gospel of John. Instead, it explores some of the major narratives and themes of the book. The next chapter, for example, is a reflection on John 1:35-42.

Your grasp of John's Gospel will be immeasurably deepened, however, if you read the entire Gospel as you work through this book. In preparation for the next chapter, read John 1:19-42, not just verses 35-42, which form the focus of discussion. Prior to chapter 3, follow the same procedure: read all the verses up to and including the specific text under discussion—that is, read John 1:43—2:11, not just 2:1-11, the focus of chapter 3. Proceed in the same fashion as you work through this book.

Trust me; if you read this book while failing to read John's Gospel, you will have traded the wonder of peering into a star-studded night for a book on astronomy. An astronomy book is only valuable if it deepens your appreciation of the heavens.

Although at times, the author paraphrases freely, except where otherwise specified, the Scripture texts cited in this book are taken from the New Revised Standard Version of the Bible. Use that or another reliable modern translation for your study Bible. The New International Version and the New American Standard Version are also good choices.

Consider first John 1:19–12:50. Following the prologue (1:1-18)—an eloquent introduction to the major themes of his Gospel—John turns to telling the story of Jesus' ministry. He emphasizes various "signs" that reveal God's saving presence in Jesus and the growing controversy with the religious authorities. By chapter 12, the continental divide of the Fourth Gospel, Jesus turns toward his cross. At that point the Gospel turns increasingly inward as Jesus struggles to articulate his unique mission to his disciples.

For now, prepare yourself for some action and adventure.

CHAPTER 2

What Does Jesus See in You?

John 1:35-42

It's every parent's nightmare. A daughter, bright and beautiful, brings home a boy to meet the folks—but he is nothing like the boy of the *parent's* dreams. His hair is long and stringy, his baseball caps says "Budweiser," and his Harley is parked out front. The daughter presents him as though he were royalty, her voice tingling with excitement. "Mom, Dad, this is . . ."

The boy puts out his hand and says, "Pleased to meetcha."

Mom shoots Dad a frantic look that says, "Dear God, *no!*" Dad looks at the boy's extended hand as though it were radioactive waste. Finally, summoning both his manners and his courage, Dad shakes the outstretched hand, feigning a politeness he does not feel.

The daughter, feeling the ice in the room, looks crushed, then defiant as her hurt hardens into resolve. Taking her new love by the arm, she draws him close and says, "Well, we have to be going."

They turn to leave as two mortified parents look after them. A moment later the roar of the motorcycle erupts, and Dad's muscles tense at the sound. Mom collapses on the couch, shaking her head. Then she voices the question that will haunt them for days, if not for months and years: "What in the world does she see in *him?*"

As parents who have lived that nightmare can attest, often the daughter sees something in her beloved that is not there.

She is in love with a fantasy that has no basis in fact. And hopefully, before being hurt too deeply, she will realize her error.

But sometimes the daughter really does see in her new love some promise or potential that a quick, cursory glance will not reveal. Sometimes, peering past the surface, she can see a Prince Charming where anxious parents see only a frog. Sometimes—not often, but *sometimes*—the daughter really does sees a diamond in the rough that her love will help polish into a thing of beauty.

When Jesus first met Simon Peter, he saw something in that brawny fisherman that no one had ever seen before: he saw the possibility of a courageous, principled man hewn from stone. Peering past surface appearances, Jesus saw clear down into Simon's soul.[1] He looked past the bluff and bravado to catch sight of the real person hidden deep within. Looking at him with a deep, penetrating gaze, Jesus saw not only what Simon was, but what by the grace of God, he *might become.*

And then Jesus gave Simon a nickname to remind him of his promise. He said that someday Simon would be known as "Peter," the Greek word for "rock." In Jesus' company this impulsive fisherman would become a man of granite. To paraphrase, Jesus said to him, "Right now people call you 'Simon,' but when I'm done with you, they'll call you 'Rocky'" (1:42).

To say the least, it was remarkable that Jesus saw in this flighty fisherman one as steady as a rock. The portrait of Simon in the Gospels shows no early signs of promise. Instead, he comes off as a blustering, reckless character, quick to speak and slow to think. Usually, when Simon Peter makes an appearance in the Gospels, he has his foot in his mouth.

At the Mount of Transfiguration, when Jesus' heavenly glory was revealed, Simon ran around like a rock-star groupie trying to get an autograph (Mark 9:2-7). Thoroughly perturbed,

---

[1] The Greek word underlying our English translation is *emblepsas.* It means a deep, penetrating gaze. It is the same word used of John's discerning look at Jesus in John 1:36 and of Jesus looking intently at the rich young ruler in Mark 10:21. The Jerusalem Bible best picks up this nuance in John 1:42, saying that when Jesus met Simon, "Jesus *looked hard at him."*

the Almighty finally thundered from the heavens, "This is my Son, the Beloved; listen to him!" (v. 7).

At Caesarea Philippi it was Simon who blurted out the words that sounded like music in Jesus' ears: "You are the Messiah, the Son of the living God" (Matthew 16:16). But only moments later that same Simon was coaching Jesus on how to "win friends and influence people" without facing his cross. Unnerved by Simon's sudden reversal, Jesus unleashed the scathing rebuke, "Get behind me, Satan!" (v. 23).

And, of course, it was Simon who brashly promised as the cross loomed near, "Lord, though all the rest desert you, I'll stand by you till the end!"

Knowing how shallow ran such sentiments, Jesus solemnly warned his cockiest disciple, "Before the cock crows, you will deny me three times" (Matthew 26:33-35).

No, before Jesus Christ completely changed Simon's life, Simon showed no sign of becoming the "Rock Man." But Jesus looked past Simon's problems to see his promise. Then he gave him a new name to signal the person he would become.

Colonel George Washington Goethals was the engineer who oversaw completion of the Panama Canal. As that awesome project unfolded, Goethals faced withering attacks from naysayers who called the venture a boondoggle and predicted its failure. Besides contending with Panama's oppressive heat and jungle forests, Goethals had to endure the carping of his many critics back home. Still, he steadfastly stuck to his task and said nothing.

Finally, one of his subordinates asked in exasperation, "Aren't you going to answer your critics?"

"In time," Goethals answered.

"How?" asked the exasperated aide.

"With the canal," said Goethals quietly. "With the canal."[2]

Fortunately, that is the tack our Lord takes with us. Jesus doesn't see us merely as we are. Rather, he sees what we might become in his presence. He sees not only our failings, but also

---

2 *Pastor's Story File 9*, no. 9 (July 1993), 8.

our promise. He sees not only our weaknesses, but also our strengths. He sees not only that which is ugly and mean, but that which is noble and good. Then he invites us into a journey of discipleship where he can set free the best that lies within us.

When Andrew and another disciple first approached Jesus, the Master asked them, "What are you looking for?" (John 1:38). That was not a casual question asked in passing. Rather, Jesus was asking what they hoped to learn about God and themselves in his company.

The two of them fumbled for an answer because the truth was, they didn't have a clue. They just knew Jesus stirred to life within them an ache and a hunger for God. So instead of answering Jesus' probing question, they asked a question of their own: "Rabbi, where are you staying?" which was their way of saying, "Lord, we really don't know what we're looking for. We just want to know *you*." So Jesus extended the simple yet potent summons, "Come and *see*."

This is also Jesus' invitation to us: "Come and see." No hard sell, no high-pressure tactics, just a gracious invitation to discover who he is and who we might become because of him. Unlike the sweating televangelist, frantic for a decision now, Jesus is supremely confident. He's in no hurry. He doesn't fear a long, careful examination. Instead, he invites it. "Why don't you risk getting close to me?" says Jesus. "Open yourself to my presence, test my claims, ask the hard questions. *For I am the light of the world. Whoever follows me will never walk in darkness*" (John 8:12).

In John Bunyan's epic work, *Pilgrim's Progress,* Evangelist points across a wide field. "Do you see yonder gate?" he asks Pilgrim.

"No," Pilgrim answers.

"Then do you see yonder shining light?"

"Yes," says Pilgrim, "I think I do."

"Then keep that light in your eye," Evangelist answers. "Keep that light in your eye."

This is the nature of Christian discipleship. It is first of all a pilgrimage. Jesus makes the offer, "Come and see," and we take a chance on him. We stumble after his light as best we can.

We follow slowly and unsteadily at first, like a toddler learning to walk, then with greater resolve and stride, until in time that hint of light up ahead yields to the fullness of the dawn and suddenly we can't help but see ourselves and our world in his light.

For us, as for those first disciples, there are few if any instantaneous transformations, just a growing apprehension of who Jesus is and of who we can become because of him. As at the beginning, so today: knowing Jesus begins with the willingness to go on a pilgrimage with him.

But there was another factor in Jesus' transformation of Simon the simpleton into Peter the rock. And that was the way Jesus used even Simon's missteps and failings to achieve his purpose. Simon was notorious for his blundering, for his failures, like his person, were large and grandiose. Many times in his journey with Jesus the fisherman turned disciple would stumble and fall. But somehow an ever-gracious Lord turned even Peter's massive mistakes toward the purpose of sculpting the "Rock Man" from an often weak, vacillating soul.

Shortly before Jesus' crucifixion, he warned his brash disciple, "Simon, Simon, Satan has asked to sift you as wheat. But I have prayed for you, Simon, that your faith may not fail. And when you have turned back, strengthen your brothers" (Luke 22:31-32, NIV). And so it happened. For though Peter failed miserably in this, his greatest test—denying his Lord three times—Jesus drew out of that very failure a promising new beginning. When Simon's cowardice got the best of him, he was devastated and ashamed, but in time Jesus drew from that chastened, humbled soul a man of dauntless courage.

Perhaps reflecting on that very experience, Peter would later write in the first of two New Testament letters bearing his name, "Rejoice, even if now for a little while you have had to suffer various trials, so that the genuineness of your faith—being more precious than gold that, though perishable, is tested by fire—may be found to result in praise and glory and honor when Jesus Christ is revealed" (1 Peter 1:6-7). So it was that in Christ's able hands, Simon's trials became a refining fire that purified and strengthened his person.

An art museum in Florence, Italy, features four figures carved by Michelangelo for the tomb of Pope Julius. The sculptures appear unfinished. The figures are emerging from rough stone blocks, as though wresting free of the rock cubes that have long held them captive. One observer notes, "In allowing us to see the cost of their creation, Michelangelo has revealed the cost of *our* creation."[3] For like ourselves, those figures are taking shape not *despite* the hammer blows directed against them, but precisely *because* of them.

When undergoing a severe testing or trial, we are apt to think the world—and perhaps God—has turned against us. But in truth, when life hammers us in that fashion, our Lord uses those blows to chip away at what is limiting the full expression of our person. And while we fear the experience will reduce us to bits, often amid the destruction and the rubble, some lost, forgotten part of the self starts coming into view. Some inner strength we had not claimed is asserted, and some faith not needed before is found. A false facade is chipped away, and a distorted view of ourselves as inept and inadequate is shattered. And in time the person we most truly are comes more clearly into focus.

Even so, some measure of suffering seems essential to that process by which God shapes and sculpts a soul. In other words, in the journey with Jesus nothing is wasted. Thankfully, he is not limited to using our strengths and successes. Rather, he uses even our weakness and our failures to transform us after his likeness.

Finally, it was the resurrection of Jesus that completed the transformation of Simon the nitwit into Peter the rock. Before the resurrection Simon was crushed by his grief, shame, and desperation. But after the resurrection Jesus sought out his beaten, beleaguered disciple by the sea (see John 21:15-19). Once more he peered deep into the broken man's eyes. "Simon son of John, do you love me?"

"Yes, Lord," Simon answered; "you know that I love you."

---

3 H. A. Williams, *True Resurrection* (New York: Holt, Rinehart, and Winston, 1972), 145.

But twice more Jesus pressed the question home, twisting it like a dagger until finally Simon was overcome by the painful memory of his denials. "Lord, you *know* everything," he cried; "you *know* that I love you!"

"Then feed my sheep," said the Master. "Feed my sheep."

On that fateful day by the Sea of Galilee, Jesus pointedly used his disciple's given name, Simon, and not his name of promise, Peter, the Rock. But several weeks later at Pentecost, Simon rose to his calling. Steeled by the assurance of his Lord's victory over sin and death, and filled with the power of the Holy Spirit, he proclaimed new life through Jesus Christ. As a result of his preaching, three thousand were added to the Church's ranks that very day (Acts 2:41). And in the days that followed, the number of new disciples continued to swell.

Alarmed at the impact this reborn Simon was having, the authorities hauled him in for questioning. They demanded that he speak no more about Jesus, for this resurrection talk was creating quite a stir. But with iron in his heart and fire in his soul, Peter answered for all who had been made new by the risen Lord: "Whether we should obey God or men, you decide. But we cannot help but speak of what we have seen and heard!" (cf. Acts 4:19-20).

The authorities were flabbergasted by the boldness of this unlettered fisherman and his companion, John. How could they stand fearless and unbowed before an imposing panel of judges assembled to stare them down? Then realization dawned. These men had been with Jesus! (Acts 4:13) Nothing else could explain the utter transformation that had come over them. For standing steady and unshaken before the highest Jewish tribunal in the land was... the *Rock Man!*

After that, no one called him "Simon" anymore. Forever after, people would call him by the name of promise Jesus gave him at the beginning—"Peter, the Rock."

When Jesus first gazed upon Simon, he saw not only what he *was*, but what by the grace of God he might become. What does Jesus see in you? For he looks at you as he looked at Simon, with a deep, penetrating gaze. He sees the potential you've never quite been able to tap. He sees the promise you've never been able to claim. And, yes, he sees the shame you've never been able to vanquish.

Do not fear Jesus' all-searching eyes, for he looks at you not in accusation, but in longing and in love. He longs to set free that beautiful person perhaps even you have forgotten is hidden deep inside!

No matter. Jesus hasn't forgotten. He knows who you are. Even now your name of promise is on his lips.

Listen to your heart, and you may hear it. Stagger after his light, and you will see. For all who keep the light of Jesus Christ in their eye will discover not only the wonder of his person, but the radiant miracle of their own.

Beyond our every pretense and shame, O Lord,
help us see the person you would have us to be.
Whisper our name of promise. Then set us free
by the power of your risen life.
Amen.

Questions for Reflection

1. What gave Jesus the capacity to see in others their untapped potential or hidden self? Have you known someone with a similar power of discernment? What kind of person was he or she?
2. What does Jesus' gentle invitation "Come and see" suggest about the Church's ministry of evangelism?
3. In what ways is following Jesus more a pilgrimage than a stopping place? What other metaphors for the life of discipleship speak to you?
4. How have you changed since beginning the journey of discipleship? What were the formative forces in your own process of transformation?
5. Can you remember a time when one of your own failures or mistakes, in time, made you a better person? What is needed for that to happen?

6. What is your own name of "promise"—a name that encapsulates the person you hope to be?
7. How might deepening your own life with Christ help that person to blossom?

CHAPTER 3

Leave It There

John 2:1-11

In the era and neighborhood where I grew up, "stay-at-home" moms were still the norm. Back then, in a slower, simpler time, parenting was not as complicated as it is today. Basically, it came down to the shrewd exercise of the good cop–bad cop syndrome.

Mom was the good cop, full of attentive concern for the children in her care. She did her best to keep two or three kids entertained, refereeing their fights and bandaging their knees, while Dad was off earning a living. But as the day wore on and Mom's nerves wore thin, she grew more stressed in her efforts to control a sometimes unruly brood. And if at that point one of the kids did something really obnoxious, Mom sometimes resorted to that most dreaded of summons: "Just you wait till your *father* gets home!"

It was a terrible thing for a wayward child to know that, shortly after arriving home, Daddy would hear Mom's horror stories and be filled with avenging wrath.

Back in those days, had I said something to my mother remotely resembling what Jesus said to his mother in the second chapter of John, I would have been taking my life in my hands. For when Mary said politely enough, "Son, they're out of wine," Jesus replied, "What's that to you and me, woman?" A crack like that would have turned my daddy into a veritable King Kong.

Frankly, despite all the ingenuity of the translators, Jesus' remark remains very pointed in the Greek. It's as though a tactful mom said to her teenager, "Son, your room still isn't picked up," and the son, looking sullen, shot back, "*Soooo?*" The Living Bible tries to clean up Jesus' remark by translating it, "I can't help you now. It isn't yet my time for miracles." But that isn't a translation; that's a coverup. The King James is much closer to the original: "Woman, what have I to do with thee? mine hour is not yet come."

Hearing Jesus address his own mother with the impersonal word *woman* grates on our ears. Some translators insert the word *mother* in the text to soften the blow, but that word isn't present. Here, Jesus explicitly calls Mary not "mother," but "woman." It's the same way he addresses her at the close of John's Gospel. From his cross, Jesus calls to Mary, standing beside the beloved disciple: "'*Woman*, here is your son.' Then he said to the disciple, 'Here is your mother'" (John 19:26-27).

Imagine the hurt in Mary's eyes when Jesus called her not "Mom," but "woman." Did she tear up in sadness? Did her mouth fall open in shock? Did her pained expression elicit any sympathy from Jesus? Surely the air was electric with tension and misunderstanding.

But Jesus didn't jump in to rescue her. He left her dangling, though his own heart was breaking at the sight of her bewilderment and pain. For the time had come for her to know and love him in a new way. She could no longer pull rank on him, claiming special privileges as his mother. She who had borne and nurtured him and held him dear would have to let him go that he might belong to the ages.

In one of his books, Lewis Smedes relates a testy conversation with his wife, Doris. She was angry because he shielded her from some disappointing news about one of their children. Smedes tried to justify his action by saying she had been through a lot lately and he didn't want to hurt her. "Let *me* decide how much hurt I can stand," Doris shot back. "I don't need you to protect me from reality."[1]

---

[1] Lewis Smedes, *A Pretty Good Person* (San Francisco: Harper Books, 1991), 80.

Trying to protect loved ones from reality is always a losing game, for sooner or later the truth catches up with you; and generally speaking, the sooner you face a difficult or unpleasant reality, the better. As Jesus' testy conversation with his mother suggests, sometimes love is better served by being painfully honest than continuing to pretend.

Even so, Jesus' abruptness with Mary was meant to pierce her illusions. He could not remain her doting son, for God's call had sounded in his life. And while it was no doubt painful for Jesus and his mother to negotiate a new relationship, he was trying to spare her an even greater pain in the future. For in time she would see: Mary had to lose a son in order to gain a Savior.

Given this awkward exchange, one might expect Mary to go away and sulk or perhaps to find some busybody with whom to commiserate: "Did you hear what he said to me, his own *mother?*" But instead, motioning the servants near, she whispered, "Do whatever he tells you." For despite Jesus' rebuff, she still had utter confidence in him. Nothing he said could deter her from leaving the problem of the wine running out in his very capable hands.

I wonder what Jesus thought as he stood there after his mother so deftly left him holding the bag. She went padding off into the far reaches of the house to reassure the hostess, "Don't worry. Everything's under control." Meanwhile, Jesus was left pondering how to be true to his own calling in the face of a domestic disaster.

He had told her, "My hour has not yet come," which meant he was not ready to reveal God's unique hold on his life.[2] But to run out of wine at a wedding reception was a terrible embarrassment. And because the bride and the groom were probably members of Jesus' own family or his intimate circle of friends, he couldn't bear to see them humiliated by having their wine run out before the party did. His love and compassion deeply stirred, Jesus simply was not free to do nothing.

---

[2] For other appearances of this phrase in John's Gospel, see 7:30; 8:20; 12:23,27; 13:1; 17:1.

The infuriating thing was that good, gentle Mary, who appeared so innocent, knew exactly what she was doing! She might not fully understand her son, but she knew his heart. She knew he could not remain unmoved in the face of a pressing need. So she promptly dropped the dilemma squarely in Jesus' lap and left it there.

That, it seems to me, is a perfect parable of what prayer ought to be: laying our dilemma before God and then leaving it there. All too often we approach prayer as though it were our job to instruct the Almighty. We fancy ourselves the coach, calling the quarterback over to the sidelines to give him the game-winning play. How easily we forget that our Lord knows best how to handle the dilemma at hand.

By contrast, those as confident in their Lord's character as Mary was can simply lay their troubles before Jesus and leave them there. As 1 Peter 5:7 implores us, "Cast all your anxiety on him, because he cares for you."

James Fowler, a noted psychologist of religion, has done ground-breaking research on the nature of faith. In one of his books, he tells about a twelve-year-old boy who grew up a devout believer in a family of atheists. Even when teased unmercifully the boy clung to his convictions.

Once someone asked the boy how the world would be different if God did not exist. He paused to reflect and then drew on his fish tank for an example. He explained that an aquarium is meant to be a perfectly balanced ecological system. The fish live off the oxygen and food generated by the plants, while the snails keep the tank clean, eating the algae. It's supposed to be a self-contained cycle requiring nothing of the owner.

"But my aquarium is not perfect," the boy explained. "Many times, I have to do something to restore the balance within it, so the fish won't die. And who knows," the boy concluded, "how much God does every day just to keep the world running, and we don't even know it."[3]

---

3 James W. Fowler, *Becoming Adult, Becoming Christian* (San Francisco: Harper & Row, 1984), 88.

Such a basic confidence toward God is the essence of faith. It was the kind of faith Mary showed when she laid her troubles before Jesus and left them there. She didn't know what kind of deliverance Jesus would bring; she just knew that even in the difficult circumstances at hand, things would soon be better because of him. Even when she didn't fully understand him, even after his sharp rebuke left wetness in her eyes and questions in her soul, she entrusted her dilemma to Jesus and *left it there*. And no doubt our own efforts to pray would be greatly enhanced if we followed her lead. For if, like Mary, we come to know and love Jesus, we will find ourselves coaching him less and trusting him more.

Once Mary had shifted the dilemma at the wedding from herself to Jesus, the problem was his to sort out. And even for him it really was a problem. For throughout his ministry Jesus refused to be reduced to a cheap trickster. In the wilderness Satan tempted him to gain a following by taking a swan dive off the pinnacle of the temple. Jesus refused then, as he refused throughout his ministry, to win adherents by sensational acts. The problem with a faith grounded in sensationalism is that it demands ever greater sensations to be maintained. Like a drug addict needing ever larger doses to get the same high, people driven by spiritual sensationalism can never get enough.

How, then, was Jesus to keep the wedding party from crashing for lack of wine without resorting to the sort of cheap stunt he despised? He did it by orchestrating his miracle offstage, out of the spotlight. First, he called the servants aside and privately told them to top off the water jugs used for ceremonial washing before meals. Once the fresh water had been poured in, Jesus told a servant to draw some off the top and take it to the head waiter. The servant did so, no doubt thinking this a strange request, for the head waiter always sampled the food and the wine but not the drinking water.

When the head waiter put the cup to his mouth, however, a broad smile spread across his face. With obvious satisfaction he smacked his lips and said, "Say, this is good stuff!"

Next the best man was given a sip. Smiling broadly, he called out to the bridegroom, "John, you've been holding out on us! You've saved the best till last!"

The bridegroom didn't really understand what was happening, but he quickly played along. He just shrugged his shoulders, feigned an all-knowing smile, and then breathed a sigh of relief. Meanwhile, the startled servant craned his neck to see what was in that cup. All the while, Jesus stayed out of view, with only his disciples—and his mama—fully comprehending what had happened. Even so, John adds the postscript: "Jesus did this, the first of his signs, in Cana of Galilee, and revealed his glory; and his disciples *believed* in him" (v. 11).

John calls this miracle a "sign."[4] That was his favorite word for Jesus' miracles, for they were "signs"—pointers or clues to the wonder of God's saving presence in Jesus Christ—but they were not decisive proof. As evidence, a skilled attorney could have torn them to shreds. Maybe Jesus paid off the servant to pull a scam. Or maybe he poured the wine in the jars himself when no one was looking. A crafty skeptic could no doubt come up with any number of possible explanations for Jesus' miracles, as during his ministry many did and many still do today.

But Mary and the disciples knew better. For as those closest to Jesus, they knew not only the miracle, but the man. They knew he wasn't some religious huckster generating a following, but the Holy Son of God laying hold of their hearts. So when they saw a disastrous situation turn around because Jesus was near, they knew what was happening. As John tells us, "They believed in him"—not merely in his miracles, but in *him*.

Still today it is because things change for the better when Jesus is around that our faith begins to grow. Whenever he is near, sagging spirits are restored and the party revived. A life

---

4 The changing of the water into wine is the first of seven "signs" in John's Gospel. The others are healing a royal official's son (4:46-54), healing a paralytic (5:1-15), multiplying the loaves (6:1-15), walking on the sea (6:16-22), healing a man blind from birth (chap. 9), and raising Lazarus from the dead (chap. 11). In the Bible, the number seven signifies completeness. The seven signs signify the fullness of God's self-disclosure in Jesus.

that had gone flat is filled with zest, and a once insipid soul becomes vital again.

There we were, crushed after someone who promised to hold us forever let us go. Nothing was left but the ache of our loneliness and guilt. But then someone put his or her arm about us in Jesus' name, and we discovered that while the marriage was over, our life wasn't. And in time we were laughing and singing and dancing up a storm at that party called the Church.

There we were with nothing but the remnants of a childhood faith shattered by the hard questions of life. We thought our spiritual journey was over, a quaint memory from a nostalgic past. But by the grace of God, a fellow pilgrim drew off some new wine for us from the old, old Story. And once more we felt the fire of God's Spirit chase the chill from our bones.

There we were staring into the impenetrable darkness of a loved one's death. It seemed grief was about to swallow us whole. But in the wee hours of the morning, when a troubled heart wouldn't let us rest, we heard the promise sound in our soul: "He who believes in me, though he die, yet shall he live" (John 11:25). And from the bitter water of fading memories came the sweet wine of our Lord's living presence.

Our Lord yet works discreetly, preferring the shadows to the spotlight. But again and again, in times of despair and desperation, things mysteriously change for the better. Some see that as the hand of fate or a stroke of luck. But when surprised by grace, the faithful know to think of him.

So don't doubt Jesus now when life has you hemmed in and feeling hopeless. Instead, bring him the problem that defies solution. Bring him the heartache that won't let you go. Bring him the dilemma that has you twisted in knots. Whatever your need or desperation, bring it to the Master and *leave it there*.

In his time and in his way, Jesus yet turns the water into wine. And like those disciples of old, we catch a glimpse of his glory and believe.

Save us from thinking that when the wine runs out
the party is over, for that just may be your opening
to renew us by the power of your living presence.

Surprise us by your grace this day and forevermore.
In your name we ask it, O Christ, to the glory of
the eternal God.
Amen.

Questions for Reflection

1. Couldn't Jesus have been a little more polite? Was such a blunt response to his mother really needed? What does the conduct of Jesus' mother in this passage suggest? Compare also Mark 3:21 and 3:31-35.
2. In declaring his independence from his mother, Jesus was negotiating a passage that in some sense every mature adult must face. In what ways was Jesus' experience of this transition like our own? In what ways was his experience unique?
3. Just before giving his disciples the Model Prayer, or Lord's Prayer (Matthew 6:9-15), Jesus said, "Do not heap up empty phrases as the Gentiles do; for they think that they will be heard because of their many words. Do not be like them, for your Father knows what you need before you ask him" (Matthew 6:7-8). If the Father already knows our needs, why pray at all?
4. How does John's use of the word *sign* illuminate your own understanding of the miraculous?
5. What kind of faith is like stagnant water kept in urns? What kind of faith is like wine?
6. Can you relate a crisis from your own experience when the "wine ran out" but Jesus—or his body, the Church— turned the water into wine? What were the dynamics of that transformation?

CHAPTER 4

Sometimes There Just Aren't Enough Rocks

John 2:13-22

Just when we think we have Jesus pegged, he goes and pulls a stunt like the cleansing of the temple. Let's face it: this unseemly display doesn't square at all with the popular view of Jesus as meek and mild and utterly nonthreatening. Here we see a fearsome Jesus, his blood boiling with righteous indignation, brandishing a whip. The only mention this scandalous scene got in my Sunday school education was as a proof text for not having bake sales in the church. Somehow, Jesus' white-hot anger got missed in the telling of the tale.

Perhaps the Gospel writers also found this incident embarrassing, but if so, they refused to soft-pedal it. Each included this startling episode of Jesus looking more like Wyatt Earp at the OK Corral than Mahatma Gandhi. Matthew, Mark, and Luke each placed it at the end of Jesus' ministry, where chronologically it almost certainly belongs.[1] The cleansing of the temple was the opening salvo in Jesus' holy week advance on a decrepit religious establishment. But John, with the poetic license that marks his work, put the cleansing of the temple at

---

[1] The other three Gospels place the cleansing of the temple immediately after Jesus' triumphal entry into Jerusalem (Matthew 21:1-13; Mark 11:1-19; Luke 19:28-46).

29

the beginning, for he rightly saw that, from the start, Jesus was on a collision course with a corrupt religious establishment. While each put his own spin on the story, the Gospel writers were careful to note what we are sometimes eager to forget: the God who confronts us in Jesus Christ is not some docile deity who winks at our moral indiscretions. Rather, the wrath of the living God is stirred by every kind of hypocrisy and exploitation, especially those cloaked in a religious guise.

When John writes that cattle, sheep, and doves were "in the temple" (2:14), many readers imagine a sanctuary teeming with animals. Anyone would be incensed at such a sight. But that is not the picture John intends, for Jerusalem's temple was not just a sanctuary, but a large complex of buildings and interlocking courtyards. And all this buying and selling was going on in the largest and outermost courtyard, the court of the Gentiles.[2]

While perhaps a bit inelegant, this marketing of animals was meant as a convenience. It allowed pilgrims from distant lands to obtain the required dove or lamb needed for a sacrifice. What was wrong with making the temple "user-friendly" by allowing worshipers to purchase needed supplies at the door?

Several things, actually. First, out-of-town visitors were being charged exorbitant rates to change their money into the local currency. Second, they were required to buy sacrifices from licensed vendors in the temple rather than at the going rate in the streets.[3] Furthermore, this noisy distraction was confined to the area where Gentiles came to worship. Considered beyond the pale of God's grace, Gentiles could not enter the temple's inner precincts. Thus, their attempts to pay homage to Israel's God were rendered irrelevant, if not impossible, by this melee.[4] In other words, what was going on in the temple wasn't a public service. It was a scam. And all of it was unfolding

---

[2] The Greek word here translated, "temple" is *hieron*, designating the entire temple compound; the inner sanctuary was *naos*, the word used in verses 19 and 21.
[3] The other three Gospel writers include Jesus' reference to the temple as a "den of robbers" (Matthew 21:13; Mark 11:17; Luke 19:46).
[4] Consider Jesus' indictment as recorded by Mark: "Is it not written, 'My house shall be called a house of prayer for *all the nations'?*" (Mark 11:17, my emphasis).

beneath the watchful eyes of the priests who could hardly wait for services to end so they could count their share of the take. To see greedy priests practicing economic exploitation and religious exclusion—on the temple premises, no less—grated on Jesus' nerves and stirred his soul. It was the sort of rank hypocrisy that made the religious elite of his day so intolerable to him. Such persons observed the fine points of the Jewish tradition while violating the spirit of Jewish teaching. As Jesus thundered against them on another occasion, "Woe to you Pharisees! For you tithe mint and rue and herbs of all kinds, and neglect justice and the love of God" (Luke 11:42).

The conventionally religious of Jesus' day thought maintaining a semblance of piety would shelter them from God's all-seeing eyes. But for Jesus, true spirituality sprang from a deeper source, namely, a heartfelt need for God's forgiveness and grace.

Indeed, when religion is used to mask rather than reveal our need for grace, it becomes a dangerous commodity. The travesty going on in the temple of Jesus' day was but a microcosm of the evils perpetrated throughout history in the name of religion run amuck. From the Inquisition to the Holocaust, selfrighteous fervor has fueled some of humanity's greatest crimes.

In his terrifying and poignant novel *Sophie's Choice*, William Styron writes about the people who staffed Hitler's concentration camps. We want to believe they were savage barbarians, evil Nazis perpetrating crimes of which we ourselves are incapable. The ugly truth is that the Holocaust was unleashed by persons just like us, people who loved their families, minded their manners, listened to Mozart, and went to church. Styron writes:

> The rolls of the SS at Auschwitz contained almost no professional soldiers but were instead composed of a cross section of German society. They included waiters, bakers, carpenters, restaurant owners, physicians, a bookkeeper, a post office clerk, a waitress, a bank clerk, a nurse, a locksmith, a fireman, a customs officer, a legal advisor, . . . The list goes on and on with these

commonplace and familiar citizens' pursuits. There
needs only to be added the observation that history's
greatest liquidator of Jews, the thick-witted Heinrich
Himmler, was a chicken farmer.[5]

Jesus saw clear through every religious pretense to the
heart of the human situation. He saw there a terrible capacity
for evil alive within us all.[6] And that capacity is most worri-
some and destructive when it is denied beneath a mask of
piety and pride. Indeed, the temple priests of Jesus' day had
turned the very house of God into a "den of thieves." But lost
in the fog of their rationalizations, they didn't even see their
crime.

Incensed by the oriental bazaar flourishing on the temple
grounds, Jesus decided to put an end to the spectacle. So in an
act of prophetic drama worthy of Amos or Elijah, he grabbed
a handful of cords and whipped them into a makeshift cat-o'-
nine-tails. Then he slapped a sheep on the hindquarters, sending it scurrying, and soon complete pandemonium broke loose.
The animals began to stampede, and shouts of protest were
raised as frantic merchants chased the beasts.

One of the money changers ran over to Jesus waving his
arms and said, "Hey, relax. It's just *business!*" whereupon the
fire in Jesus' eyes flared brighter still and he began knocking
over the money changers' tables with abandon. Frantic little
men began chasing silver and gold coins rolling about on the
floor as frightened worshipers ran for cover. Rising above the
fray, the voice of the Master sounded. "Get this junk out of
here!" he roared. "How dare you turn my Father's house into
a market!" (cf. John 2:16, NIV).

In this terrifying scene, we see Jesus putting the fear of
God into people instead of assuring them of God's love and

---

5 William Styron, *Sophie's Choice* (New York: Bantam Books, 1983), 182-83.

6 The account of the temple cleansing is followed by the haunting epilogue, "Many
   believed in his name because they saw the signs that he was doing. But Jesus on
   his part would not entrust himself to them, *because he knew . . . what was in everyone*" (John 2:23-25).

care. It is a disconcerting picture, and there is simply no way to reconcile this image with the emasculated, meek-as-Milquetoast Jesus of popular piety. Seeing God's holy temple turned into a breeding ground for greed and evil was more than Jesus could bear. Seething with righteous indignation, he boldly threw down the gauntlet to a corrupt religious establishment.

This utterly unconventional view of Jesus reminds us that there is such a thing as *redemptive* anger. When confronted by gross evil and injustice, anger can be a godly response. The Bible condemns anger that is nursed like a wound and then vented in a vindictive, destructive fashion.[7] A chaste, godly anger, however, is not only possible, but necessary, when the weak and innocent are being victimized by the strong. Most of history's greatest reforms—from the abolition of slavery to equal rights for women—have been fueled by a just and holy anger.

But we dare not turn Jesus' cleansing of the temple into carte blanche for venting anger of every kind. Most often, our anger is impulsive and self-serving, not righteous and pure. Usually, when we flare up in anger, it is not to protect the innocent, but to protect our own position and privilege.

So why are we so quick to identify *with* Jesus in this passage? Instinctively, we assume he is eager to brandish his whip on *our* behalf. But could it be that some of his ire might be directed in our direction?

Are we altogether lacking in the hypocrisy he found so appalling? Do we not have our own private little compromises with what is right and just and true? Have we never bent the rules for personal gain? Have we never countenanced some evil in our own lives, hoping our Lord wouldn't notice? The truth is, we need his cleansing as much Jerusalem's temple ever did.

But the mealy-mouthed keepers of the temple treasury didn't see it that way. After the excitement subsided, they came storming up to Jesus. "By what right have you done this?" they

---

[7] "Be angry but do not sin; do not let the sun go down on your anger" (Ephesians 4:26).

demanded. "This little tantrum of yours is going to cost us a fortune! You'd better have some kind of explanation!"

"Destroy this temple," said Jesus, "and in three days I'll raise it up" (John 2:19).

"You'll *what?*" one of the ringleaders shot back, his eyes bulging with rage. "This temple took forty-six years to build, and you—a no-count carpenter from Nazareth—will rebuild it in three days?" Pointing to the door, the spokesman said with a menacing glare, "Get out before we throw you out!"

Jesus looked in pity at the pathetic little man before him. Then unshaken and unafraid, he turned to leave.

The next day or the day after, the temple profiteers were back in force. Perhaps they were even offering deep discounts to lure back customers who had been rattled by the disturbance. Jesus' cleansing of the temple was a symbolic act without any enduring impact in itself. In no time everyone was back to business as usual.

But for Jesus the die was cast. He determined to make good on his promise of opening a new pathway to God, one not dependent on a physical temple. The cleansing so desperately needed in the human heart would come at the cost of his own life. He turned toward his cross in the confidence that what his anger couldn't conquer, his love surely would.

The movie *Forrest Gump* is best remembered for Tom Hanks' line that "life is like a box of chocolates." But for me the most gripping scene in the movie is when the leading lady, Jenny, returns to the abandoned, dilapidated farmhouse where she grew up. As she remembers the sexual abuse she endured as a child, she is overcome by remorse and anguish. Suddenly filled with rage, she begins throwing rocks at the house. The photography is gripping as Jenny picks up rock after rock, hurling each one violently at the house.

Finally exhausted, she collapses and begins to weep. Forrest sidles up beside her. Not really understanding what has happened, he says more than he knows: "Sometimes there just aren't enough rocks."

Jesus came to the same conclusion about the corrupt, decaying religious system represented by the grand larceny flourishing in the temple's wings. It could not be reformed; it would have to be demolished—not by throwing more rocks or staging further cleansings, but by offering up his own life as a sacrifice for the sins of the world. As John whispers from just offstage, "[Jesus] was speaking of the temple of his body. After he was raised from the dead, his disciples remembered that he had said this; and they believed the scripture and the word that Jesus had spoken" (2:21-22).

At the cross of Calvary, Jesus' anger and love came together in a single purifying stream. There he died to pierce forever after the blind pride of a self-satisfied religiosity. Then he rose to offer new life to all who placed their hope not in their religious pedigree, but in the transforming power of his all-sufficient grace. Now pilgrims seeking spiritual renewal would need no religious hierarchy; they would need only him. As the writer to the Hebrews expressed it, "My friends, since we have confidence to enter the sanctuary by the blood of Jesus, by the new and living way that he opened for us through the curtain (that is, through his flesh), . . . let us approach with a true heart in full assurance of faith" (10:19-22).

Yes, the cleansing of the temple signaled the end to the old order and the christening of the new, for with the coming of God's Son, the temple—the place where God was decisively present in the world—shifted from a building to the person of Jesus. Now all those who are bound to him by faith receive the gift of the Holy Spirit and become themselves a temple of God's indwelling presence.[8]

That does not mean, however, that believers are suddenly numbered among the "righteous" and can dance on the grave of Jerusalem's fallen temple. Rather, Jesus' followers are those who recognize that the ramshackle houses hiding *their own* hypocrisy and shame must come tumbling down. For only then can the living Christ help them build new lives on the purged ground of the persons they used to be.

---

[8] As Jesus said to the woman at the well, "Woman, believe me, the hour is coming when you will worship the Father neither on this mountain nor in Jerusalem . . . But the hour is coming, and now is here, when the true worshipers will worship the Father in spirit and truth" (John 4:21,23).

C. S. Lewis offers an arresting image of the transformation Christ brings in the life of the believer. Imagine you are a house, he suggests, that Christ has been asked to renovate. At first, you appreciate his efforts, for the work he is pursuing is relatively minor, like patching the leaks in the roof and unstopping the drains. But then he begins to completely revamp the house in a way that is quite disruptive and doesn't seem to make any sense at all. What on earth is he up to? Why is he adding a wing here, putting in an extra floor there, running up towers, making courtyards, and landscaping gardens?

The answer is that his blueprints are radically different from yours. You thought he was just going to remodel you into a decent little cottage, but, in fact, he is building a palace, for he intends to inhabit it himself.[9]

Jesus was and is a disconcerting presence. To know and love him is to tangle with the very same character who created such a ruckus in the temple that fateful day in Jerusalem. Those wanting a calm, uncomplicated life need not apply. But those who can bear the sting of Jesus' challenge will also experience the healing balm of his grace. For at the intersection of his truth and love, new life is found. Those who allow his anger to evoke a heartfelt repentance—and his love a fierce devotion—will find the rotting shell of a feigned selfhood shattered and an authentic person beginning to grow. In such as these, the Word made flesh in the long-ago and far-away still comes to indwell and hallow human life today.

Forgive us, O holy Christ, for the zeal
with which we pursue the sins of others.
Give us eyes to see our own need for your grace
and truth and healing. Then come in your risen presence
to indwell us and make us new.
Amen.

---

[9] C. S. Lewis, *Mere Christianity* (New York: Macmillan, 1976), 174.

Questions for Reflection

1. Are you relieved, alarmed, or both, to see Jesus angry in the temple?
2. What distinguishes a chaste, godly anger from anger that is destructive and self-serving?
3. Where are hypocrisy and greed most blatant in the religious community today? How might Jesus challenge such abuses?
4. Pascal said, "[People] never do evil so completely and cheerfully as when they do it from religious conviction." Why is religious fervor so often coupled with self-righteous arrogance and blindness?
5. How does one balance prophetic passion with an ongoing recognition of one's own need for grace?
6. Since Jesus himself is the "new temple" of Christian faith, what does that make of "sacred places"? What does it mean to speak of such a place in a world where he is everywhere present?

CHAPTER 5

The Wonder of Being "Born Again"

John 3:1-16

A sociologist visiting a tribal village raised her camera to take pictures of some children at play. Suddenly the children began yelling and waving their arms in protest. Seeing their antics, the freshly minted Ph.D. lowered her camera in embarrassment. She had forgotten, she explained to the chief, that certain tribes believed the soul is lost if one's picture is taken. She then launched into a long-winded explanation of the camera's operation. Several times the chief tried to interrupt, but to no avail.

Finally, after putting all the primitive man's fears to rest, the savvy sociologist allowed him to speak. Sporting a wide, toothy grin, he told her, "The children were trying to tell you to take the lens cap off."[1]

In Jesus' encounter with Nicodemus, we see the master teacher trying to get this super-serious Pharisee[2] to take the lens cap off. Nicodemus comes on like some kind of theological big shot, ready to match wits with a young rabbi on the rise. But throughout the whole discussion, Nicodemus fails to realize that his lens cap is on. He wants to determine the truth

---

[1] *Dynamic Illustrations*, January/February 1995, "Human Relations."

[2] The Pharisees were the most devout of Jewish sects.

about Jesus by using his superior analytical powers. As he is about to learn, he cannot "see" who Jesus is until he approaches with the unabashed honesty and wonder of a child.

John tells us Nicodemus came to Jesus "by night." Nicodemus didn't want his buddies in the religious establishment to know he was somewhat taken with the strange new teacher from Nazareth.[3] After all, Jesus didn't go to an Ivy League school, and he hadn't published in any learned journals. Still there was something about him that hooked Nicodemus's interest. As a "leader of the Jews" (3:1), Nicodemus kept an ear to the ground. And he knew that among the locals, this Jesus was creating quite a stir. Nicodemus had even stood at the edge of the crowd a time or two to hear Jesus for himself. And despite Jesus' lack of credentials, Nicodemus had to admit that every time this man opened his mouth, the Spirit of God seemed to stir. So he went to Jesus to talk a little theology and have a polite, stimulating discussion, such as one might have over a cup of coffee in the back of the Barnes and Noble bookstore.

"Rabbi," said Nicodemus, "we know you are a teacher who has come from God; for no one can do these signs that you do apart from the presence of God" (3:2).That's the usual concession made to Jesus. He's a great teacher to be sure. Given his impact on history, who could deny that? Here we see Nicodemus taking the high ground and giving Jesus his due.

But Jesus isn't impressed. Nicodemus's theological musings don't interest him. Instead, Jesus throws Nicodemus a body tackle that takes him out at the knees: "Unless you're born again, you can't see the kingdom of God." In other words, "Nicodemus, unless you get that lens cap off, you're going to remain as blind as a bat."

This isn't at all how Nicodemus intended the discussion to go. He makes a perfectly reasonable statement to Jesus—a compliment even—and Jesus comes up with this? Nicodemus feels his reservations on the rise. Maybe this Jesus is a nut after all.

---

[3] In addition to the practical necessity for Nicodemus's nocturnal visit, "night" is full of symbolic meaning. For John it signifies the darkness of unbelief: "The light shines in the darkness, but the darkness has not understood it" (1:5, NIV).

"How can one who is old be born again?" asks Nicodemus. Then, in an attempt at humor, he adds, "Surely he cannot enter a second time into his mother's womb to be born!" (3:4, NIV).

"Something like that," says Jesus, nodding. "Only it's not your mama's womb you need to reenter, but the womb of God."

To be "born again."[4] Strip away all the pious abuse the words have suffered. Forget those who chirp about being "born again" as though it were a badge of honor. Break through the religious encrustations that have buried the words and hear the phrase for the terrifying summons it is. For here Jesus is talking about becoming small and vulnerable and balling ourselves up into the fetal position and entrusting ourselves to God. For a living faith isn't birthed when we are feeling all cocksure and strong. Most often it takes shape as we dare to come to Jesus with the vulnerability and need of a child.

A little girl named Megan—not quite six—accompanied her mother to an art show devoted to the works of a local potter. As Megan was led through the display of beautiful, exotic pieces, her mother kept telling her not to touch anything. "The pieces are 'fragile,'" her mom kept repeating. "They break very easily."

When the two of them finished strolling through the gallery, they were met by the potter, a family friend. He leaned down to speak with Megan. "What did you think of the show?" he asked.

Casting a furtive glance at her mother, she put her mouth to his ear and whispered, "May I touch the 'fragile' things?"[5]

As would a child, many of us ache to touch the "fragile things": the hunger for God—who once seemed so real—before a growing cynicism snatched it away; the longing to be loved just for who we are, like a baby cuddled at her mama's breast; the yearning to be spontaneous and free, as when spring meant bare feet and fall meant a kite.

---

4 The word translated "born again" (NIV) can also be translated "born from above" (NRSV). In all likelihood, John intended both meanings. From the perspective of the believer, coming to faith in Jesus is like being "born again." From the perspective of eternity, such a new beginning comes "from above" (3:13-16).

5 Laurie Beth Jones, *Jesus CEO, Using Ancient Wisdom for Visionary Leadership* (New York: Hyperion, 1995), 223-24.

But all the while, our grown-up, Nicodemus-self is slapping that would-be child on the wrist. "Grow *up*," he says. "Act your age." "Be careful." "Watch your back." For the world is a dangerous place. And if people know the truth about you, they won't love you anymore.

Jesus calls Nicodemus's way of being in the world being born "of the flesh" (3:6). It is to live only at the level of one's adult, rational self, leaving that anxious, driven soul in charge and calling the shots. But spiritual rebirth—being "born of the Spirit"—begins at a different place. It begins when a person quits trying to be all grown-up and self-important and comes to God as child seeking refuge at his mother's lap: "Unless you come to me as a little child," says Jesus, "you can't enter my kingdom" (Matthew 18:3).

When people come to Jesus in their vulnerability and need, a miracle happens. They receive "power"—in the words of John's prologue—"to become children of God" (1:12). For the Spirit enters their lives in a radically new way, and they begin to live out of a new center: the peace and presence of God. This results in a transformation so thoroughgoing and complete, it can only be described as a new birth.[6]

But Nicodemus, all uptight and out of touch, can't fathom what Jesus is talking about. To him a spiritual rebirth is not an enchanting possibility; it is a theological problem. So he keeps pursuing the "how" questions: "*How* can one who is old be born again?" "*How* can these things be?" But Jesus dodges the "how" questions by appealing to the mystery of the wind.[7]

"It's like the wind, Nicodemus. Remember when you were a kid and you ran through the wind with your arms flapping, imagining you could fly? You didn't have a clue where that

---

[6] John's preferred language for the transformation in the life of the believer is that of the new birth (1 John 4:7; see also 1 Peter 1:23 and Titus 3:5). By contrast, Paul's central metaphor for this radical new beginning is dying and rising with Christ (Romans 6:1-7; Galatians 2:20).

[7] The Greek has a wordplay here that is not picked up by our English translations; the Greek word for "wind"—*pneuma*—is also the word for "spirit." "The wind/Spirit blows where it chooses. . . . So it is with everyone who is born of the wind/Spirit" (3:8).

wind came from, but it set your spirit soaring, and you thought it might lift you up, all the way to God! Well, that's what it's like to be born again."

But Nicodemus just looks at Jesus in a dull stupor, no hint of recognition in his eyes. Seeing the blank stare, Jesus shakes his head in wonderment. "I can't believe you're a respected religious teacher, Nicodemus. I have friends who are four-year-olds who know more about God than you."

At this point, Nicodemus fades from the scene. And while there are hints later in John's Gospel that the wind of the Spirit finally caught up with him and mussed his hair and stirred his soul,[8] for now Nicodemus remains the detached intellectual who is spiritually blind. John grabs the microphone to tell us who Jesus really is because he doesn't want us to miss it as Nicodemus did.

"No one has ascended into heaven except the one who descended from heaven, the Son of Man" (3:13). In other words, Jesus is not merely a "teacher from God," as Nicodemus said. Jesus is the very light of God spilling into a dark, contorted world.

And when that broken world crucified God's one and only Son, God didn't strike back in savage anger. Rather, God's own heart submitted to being broken on the hard wood of the cross, and from the anguish of that unspeakable love flowed the salvation of the world. "For God *so loved* the world that he gave his only Son, so that everyone who believes in him may not perish but may have eternal life" (3:16).

Where can we find the courage to retire our Nicodemus routine and come out of hiding? Nowhere, save at the cross of Christ, for there we discover that there is no need to hide. A God who would go to such extraordinary lengths to love us isn't about to stop just because we make a mistake, blow an opportunity, or fail to measure up. Rather, as the children of Israel were saved from a plague of snakes by gazing upon a bronze serpent fashioned by Moses (Numbers 21:4-9), so believers are saved from the poison of self-condemnation by looking to the Savior.

---

8 See John 7:50-51 where Nicodemus speaks up for Jesus and 19:39 where he assists with Jesus' burial.

This is what distinguishes Christian faith from the hysterical effort so prevalent in our culture to love ourselves into wholeness. But we can never love ourselves aright until we have been loved unconditionally by another. And one looks in vain for that caliber of love until one looks at last, in desperation and longing, to Christ suspended from his cross. For at the cross of Christ, the love of God took the worst a broken world could hurl against it. Jesus died in that hellish assault, but God's love did not. Rather, on Easter morning God's love proved stronger than the world's hate, and God's life proved stronger than the world's death.

Some years ago I was teaching a discipleship class for older children. The innocence of their younger years was waning, and like Nicodemus, they had no shortage of questions. "Are Jesus and God the same?" "Where is Jesus now? Does he live with God or in our hearts?" "Why did people kill Jesus?"

For a while, I answered the barrage of questions as best I could. But seeing the discussion was lingering too long on an abstract plane, I pulled out a book of Christian art and began showing some of Christendom's most moving depictions of Jesus on his cross.

Suddenly all the chatter and noise of a few moments before melted into the hallowed silence of eight children encountering Jesus on his cross. Their attention stayed riveted to page after page as they saw Christ pinioned to his cross like a butterfly from one of their school projects stuck to cardboard with pins. With reverence I watched the awe on their faces and the repulsion and the sadness as they pondered the nails piercing his palms, the crown of thorns pricking blood from his brow, and his body slumping beneath the sin of the world. At last neither I nor they could bear the pictures any longer. So we left the book and our classroom behind and sought refuge in that room so aptly called a sanctuary.

Sitting before a huge cross that hung from the front wall of the church, we talked about why Christians feel such a debt of gratitude when they remember that Jesus died for them. Then I pulled out my guitar and taught them the old spiritual "Were You There When They Crucified My Lord?" When they raised their voices on the chorus, "Sometimes it causes me to tremble, *tremble, TREMBLE,*" I think maybe some of them did. But I cannot say for sure, for my own head was bowed and my eyes fighting tears as from some place deep within I shuddered in wonder at what Jesus had done for me.

It was as Jesus promised: "I, when I am lifted up from the earth, will draw all people to myself" (John 12:32). Ultimately, it wasn't his teaching, his miracles, or his charm. It was his death on a Roman cross that broke our hearts and allowed the love of God to reach, bless, and heal a frightened, wounded self.

Do you want to be born again? Then don't come to Jesus as if you've got your act together. He sees straight through that Nicodemus routine. Instead, come to him out of the nakedness of your need. Come to him as that scolded child who longs to touch the fragile things. Come to him as that little girl or boy who longs to be nestled in the arms of God.

When you do, the doors of God's kingdom will swing open wide, and the wind of the Spirit will begin to blow. Christ's presence and love will infuse the depths of your being. And you, by a sheer gift of grace, will be born again.

Gracious God, forgive us our rigid, controlling ways.
Rather, may the living Christ free us to find
safe refuge in your love. Make us yours daughters
and sons by the power of your indwelling presence.
In Jesus' name we ask it.
Amen.

Questions for Reflection

1. Jesus says one must be born of "water and the Spirit" (3:5). Does water refer to the birth water of a physical birth or the baptismal waters signifying the new birth? Interpreters are divided. What does the flow of the conversation suggest to you?

2. What is the difference in being child*like* and being child*ish*? Contrast Jesus' teachings about becoming as a little child and being born again with Paul's comment in 1 Corinthians 13:11.
3. Can you remember a time you felt vulnerable and small and God was especially near? How does that experience illuminate Jesus' encounter with Nicodemus?
4. There's a lot of talk these days about "healing the child within." Is such a healing even possible apart from the gospel?
5. Is talk of being born again refreshing or offensive to you? Can you suggest other images signifying the new life Christ brings?
6. Is the cross of Christ central to your own consciousness of the love of God? Why or why not?
7. Why was Nicodemus unwilling—or unable—to meet Jesus on Jesus' terms? Do you know anybody like that? Are you such a person?

CHAPTER 6

Living Water

John 4:1-42

It was noon, and the sun—at the height of its powers—was beating down. Beads of perspiration popped up in protest, but she pressed on. Soon she would reach Jacob's well, and a cool drink of water would refresh her.

The well was always deserted at noon when all sensible people were indoors. The other women came early, in the cool of the day to draw water and swap gossip. Naturally, a woman of ill repute wasn't welcome at this social event. So she made her daily trek to the well alone when the sun was at its peak.

Climbing the last hill, her pace quickened as she neared her destination. Soon her fiery thirst would be quenched and her sagging strength renewed. Perhaps even her troubled mind would find a bit of rest.

When she topped the last summit and saw the well, her spirits fell; for there, spoiling her oasis, was a stranger. Obviously exhausted, he looked harmless enough. But her checkered history with men made her suspicious. Sweet and loving one minute, they could be cruel and vicious the next. She approached the well with caution.

The man was peering into the well, lost in his thoughts. When she drew near, he glanced up. He looked at her with warm, searching eyes, not the lusty leer so often turned in her direction. Strangely, she felt safe in his presence. But then a second look told her he was Jewish. The realization made her skin crawl. As a Samaritan, she hated and despised the Jews.

The feud between Samaritans and Jews was centuries old, and the bad blood ran deep.[1]

She decided to draw her water quickly before beating a hasty retreat. Unrolling a water bag sewn from animal skins, she lowered it one hundred feet into Jacob's well. When she pulled the bag back up, it was stretched tight and glistening. Seeing that the stranger had no flask, she denied herself the pleasure of taking a drink right away. Instead, she poured the water into a jug and turned to leave. Once out of sight, she would take the first long, satisfying swig.

"Mind if I have a drink?" the stranger called after her.

The woman froze, not believing her ears. Jews and Samaritans didn't share words, much less the mouth of a common jug. It was as unthinkable as a white in the Old South drinking from a water fountain reserved for blacks.

"Come on, mister," said the woman, a bit wary now. "You know Jews and Samaritans don't mix."

"Maybe not," said the stranger. "But if you knew who was speaking to you, you'd ask for living water."

"And just where are you going to get this *living water?*" asked the woman, her suspicions rising. "You don't even have a water bag, and the well is deep."

"Doesn't matter," said the stranger. "For the water I give will become a spring within, gushing up to eternal life."

The woman's curiosity was aroused. Had this stranger discovered a babbling brook or spring that might spare her the wearying trek to the well? Swallowing her pride, she pressed for details. "Sir, give me some of this water so I don't have to keep coming here to drink."

Living water. It's an enchanting phrase suggesting something mysterious, magical, and mighty. Indeed, Jesus says this water will burst forth as a fountain in the soul, quenching the deepest yearnings of the human spirit (4:13-14). Clearly Jesus

---

1 The hostilities between Jews and Samaritans dated from the period after the fall of Samaria in 722 B.C.E. Jews in the northern kingdom eventually intermarried with their conquerors, the Assyrians. Their neighbors to the south regarded such Israelites as "half-breeds."

was talking about something more than ordinary water. As was typical of him, he often drew from the routine a deeper, spiritual meaning. But the woman at the well heard him—initially, at least—at the literal level only.

In chapter 7, however, John nestles an important footnote to this story. There the striking phrase "living water" appears again, and Jesus more fully reveals its meaning. This telling incident occurred as the temple priests poured water over the altar in an elaborate ceremony. At that strategic moment, Jesus cried, "Let anyone who is thirsty come to *me*, and let the one who believes in me drink. As the scripture has said, 'Out of the believer's heart shall flow rivers of *living water.*'" And just in case we still don't get it, John tells us plainly, "Now he said this about the Spirit, which believers in him were to receive" (John 7:37-39).

Thus, by "living water" Jesus means the indwelling presence of God in the life of the believer. And unlike well water that must be drawn again and again, this living water forms an unfailing fountain in the soul. It is the very Spirit of God bubbling up to "eternal life."[2]

Yet like that Samaritan woman of old, many of us are burned out, dried up, and bone weary. We've never discovered this spring of spiritual vitality welling up from within. Instead, we've tried to sustain our faith by drawing from somebody else's well. We've read this expert and that. We've bounced from church to church, or channel-hopped our way through the televangelists, searching for answers. Maybe we cloned our parent's faith or, being of a rebellious bent, tried to find its opposite, but we've not yet found our own spiritual center.

Billy Graham once told of a young man who said, "I have lost my faith."

"No," Graham answered. "You have lost your *parent's* faith. Now go and get a faith of your own."[3]

---

2 "Eternal life" in John's Gospel means far more than "life without end." It means the eternal life of God experienced in the here and now among those who believe. As Jesus says it in John 10:10, "I came that they may have life, and have it *abundantly.*"

3 Quoted in *The Christian Ministry,* September/October 1988, 22.

Finding a faith of one's own is the heart of the spiritual quest, the longing for a deep, vital, *personal* faith. At one level, this is what Jesus' encounter with the woman at the well is about. He is inviting her—and us—to stop seeking spiritual sustenance outside the self by encountering God's living presence within. Surely the Samaritan woman said more than she realized when she exclaimed, "Sir, give me this water, that I may not thirst, nor come here to draw," for that is the prayer of many a parched and weary soul.

Suddenly the story takes a surprising turn. Instead of granting the woman's request, Jesus confronts her with a painful truth about herself. "Go, call your husband," he says, "and come back" (4:16).

The woman is startled and a flush of red fills her cheeks. Looking away, she searches for an answer. Deciding to hedge her bets, she answers, "I have no husband."

"I know," says Jesus, nodding. Then, playing his trump card, he adds, "As a matter of fact, you've had five husbands. And you're not married to the man with whom you're living now."

One wonders why Jesus felt the need to press the matter of her scandalous past. The woman frankly acknowledged her unmarried status. Why not tactfully let the matter drop? Why rub salt in the wound by confronting her with a string of marital failures and her current adulterous relationship?

Because if living water is to erupt in the depths of the being, one must be utterly honest with oneself and with God. Hypocrisy and self-deception are the death knell of the spiritual life.

This woman was in hiding behind a succession of barriers, like an embassy seeking protection from a terrorist attack. In order to reach her, Jesus had to step over barriers of race, religion, and gender. And every time he drew close, she threw up another barrier to stay his advance. "Are you greater than our ancestor Jacob, who gave us this well?" . . . "Should we worship in Samaria or in Jerusalem?" . . . "Someday the Messiah will come and answer all our questions." She used religion as many people use it still—to keep others at a distance. Instead of an invitation to freedom and an abundant life, religion was for her a safe place to hide.

In his book *Why Am I Afraid to Tell You Who I Am?* John Powell relates a conversation that occurred while the work was in progress. In talking with an acquaintance, Powell mentioned the title of his forthcoming book. The other person responded by asking, "Do you want an answer to your question?"

"That's the purpose of the booklet," Powell responded, "to answer that question."

"But do you want *my* answer," the other asked.

"Why, yes, of course I do," Powell answered.

"I am afraid to tell you who I am, because, if I tell you who I am, you may not like who I am, and that's all I have."[4]

Something of this fear lurks within us all. We're afraid that if others know the truth about us, they'll withhold their approval and love. So we wear masks and pretend, trying to be who we think others *want* us to be instead of being the person we are. Or like the woman at the well, we rebel against others' expectations—real and imagined—by forging lives that are ugly and self-destructive. In either event, we are terrified of being honest and real.

Yet here stands Jesus, the human embodiment of God's healing love, trying to coax this woman out of hiding. He bears in his own person a love sufficient to vanquish all her fears.[5] But she, like many of us, is not ready to believe. Still trying to evade his grace, she throws yet another theological wrench into the works: "So tell me, since you are obviously an expert. Should one worship at the mountain of the Samaritans,[6] or in Jerusalem, with the Jews?"

Jesus waves the question aside as irrelevant. "Woman, the time is coming and now is when true worshipers will worship the Father in spirit and truth."

With those revolutionary words, Jesus Christ swept aside all the irrelevancies people try to make the heart of religion. In

---

4 John Powell, *Why Am I Afraid to Tell You Who I Am?* (Niles, Ill.: Argus, 1969), 12.

5 Cf. 1 John 4:18: "There is no fear in love, but perfect love casts out fear."

6 The Samaritans worshiped at Mount Gerizim, a mountain in northern Israel.

their place he named forever after the essence of true spirituality: those who worship the living God must worship in spirit and in truth. "Spirit" points to the miracle of God's abiding presence, and "truth" points to the crucial role of honesty in the life of faith—both our honesty with God and God's honesty with us in disclosing God's own deepest, truest self in the person of Jesus Christ.[7]

Had the woman at the well merely been honest with Jesus, that might have been therapeutic. But personal honesty was not sufficient to cause living water to burst forth in her soul. For that to happen, the truth of her confession had to be met by the truth of the gospel: no matter how great one's need or desperation, God's grace is greater still.

The woman at the well couldn't know that someday Jesus would die for her sins and the sins of the whole world. But that day by Jacob's well she experienced in his person the grace that would later flow from his cross. As she would soon confess to her friends and neighbors, he not only knew everything about her (4:29), the real miracle was that he knew all the ugly details of her life and *loved her still.*

Rattled by her encounter with this gracious, unsettling man, the Samaritan woman sought a final evasion: "Well, these matters are too deep for me. Thank God, when the Messiah comes, he'll explain everything."

Jesus peered at her more closely. Seeing embers of faith glowing in her soul, he breathed words meant to stir them into flame: "I who am speaking to you am he."

Her mouth fell open, and her water jar fell to the ground. Jesus couldn't help but smile as the water she once held so precious splattered on the ground. At that very moment, Jesus' disciples returned and the woman—uncertain about what to do—took off for town. John adds the revealing touch that she left her water jar behind (4:28).

And why shouldn't she? For in Jesus Christ she met at last the only One who could quench the burning in her soul: the

---

7 "The law indeed was given through Moses; *grace and truth* came through Jesus Christ" (John 1:17).

burning to know that she mattered regardless of the mistakes she had made, the burning to know she could make a new start, no matter how checkered her past or how grievous her errors, the burning to know God's life-giving presence.

Because of a chance encounter with Jesus, that woman saw the possibility of grounding her self-worth in something more enduring than an endless succession of lovers. Standing in Jesus' light, she was able to face her shame. Basking in his love, she found the power to be healed. And somewhere en route from the well back to the village, she was a woman reborn.

In the film *All That Jazz*, the main character is a Broadway choreographer whose career is booming while his personal life is in shambles. His life is littered with broken relationships, and his health is shot from booze and drugs. Finally, he has a heart attack and is dying.

As the end draws near, he speaks to a hospital aide about his life. Drawing on an image from Hollywood, he says, "It's just a rough cut. I need more time." For him, his spent life is like a take from a movie. If he could go into the editing room and make a few changes, maybe the film could be salvaged. As it is, he is out of time, and the "rough cut" is all there is.[8]

The woman Jesus met by the well that day was a "rough cut" to be sure. Her life was in shambles and her failures tragic and grand. But before Jesus was done with her, she had a new start—not because she was allowed to revise and edit her past, but because in Jesus Christ she found a new future. Because of God's love in Christ, she knew it was safe to come out of hiding. His love shattered the shelf rock of her defiant will, and hidden beneath it was a spring of living water gushing up to eternal life.

That inner spring of God's Spirit is hidden within us all. We do not have to go to some special shrine to find it. We need only go to Jesus. For God sent the Son into the world to intercept us by our barren, empty wells that we might at last find living water for the soul.

Long ago the psalmist wrote, "As a deer longs for flowing streams, so my soul longs for you, O God" (Psalm 42:1). But in

---

8   Martin Thielen, *Getting Ready for Sunday's Sermon* (Nashville: Broadman, 1990), 113.

Jesus Christ, God has drawn near to quench that thirst (John 4:14)—not in the sense that believers never need spiritual refreshment, but in the sense that they know forevermore where to drink.

Feeling burned out, bone dry, and brittle? Then come to Jesus and drink deeply of his presence. No matter how big and barren your desert, he is the oasis. No matter how shriveled your spirit, he is the wellspring of new life.

We come to you, O Christ, with parched and weary souls.
Don't let us perish in some burning hot desert
of our own shame. Rather, be for us an oasis
of divine grace, renewal, and strength.
To the glory of the eternal God, our Creator,
Redeemer, and Sustainer we pray.
Amen.

Questions for Reflection

1. How is the "living water" of chapter 4 different from the stagnant water of chapter 2 (v. 6)? Why is "living water" or spring water a fitting metaphor of the Spirit?
2. What does it mean to worship God in "Spirit and truth" (4:23-24)? What would such worship look like in our churches today?
3. In this gripping story, Jesus deliberately challenges the reigning ethnic, sexual, and social prejudices of his day. Where are some of the "Jacob's wells" Jesus might seek out in our era?
4. The woman at the well threw up various smoke screens to protect herself against probing religious conversation (vv. 9, 12, 20, 25). What are some contemporary red herrings that serve much the same purpose? What does Jesus' handling of the woman's evasions suggest about responding in such situations today?
5. This story ends with a thoroughly "unchurched" person becoming a very effective evangelist (4:39-42). What does this suggest about the Church's ministry of evangelism?

CHAPTER 7

The Man Even Jesus Couldn't Cure

John 5:1-16

It was a junkyard of the human spirit, a place where broken bodies and dreams came to rest like spent, rusting vehicles piled up by the highway. No one went there willingly, for it was the last stop on the road to utter desperation. But after the doctors and the priests had done their best, and your blindness, paralysis, or other ailment remained, you went to Beth-zatha's Pool because there was nowhere else to go.[1]

Beth-zatha's Pool was a sort of first-century Lourdes, a place where sufferers descended in hope of healing. Tradition had it that periodically an angel stirred the waters. The first sufferer into the pool after that hint of the divine would be healed.[2] But the pool—or the angel—was stingy, and the healings were few and far between.

---

[1] The traditional name is the Pool of Bethesda, from the King James translation. The New Revised Standard Version renders the name "Beth-zatha," based on other early manuscripts of John's Gospel. The case is not airtight, however; both the New American Standard and New International Versions have "Bethesda."

[2] The tradition of the angel stirring the waters appears in the King James Version of the story at 5:3b-4. Most modern translations drop that line since it doesn't appear in the oldest manuscripts of John's Gospel. Nonetheless, some such hope of divine intervention seems implied in v. 8.

When Jesus returned to Jerusalem (5:1) after his forays into Samaria and Galilee (chap. 4), he made a beeline for that pool. The spectacle of a mass of tortured humanity waiting on a long shot from God tore at his heart. It was like seeing a mother on welfare waiting in line to spend her last five dollars on the lottery. So Jesus went to Beth-zatha's Pool to offer the possibility of healing and new life. He bore in his own person a grace and love so large that it dwarfed the alleged stirrings of God in Beth-zatha's murky waters. Those who came to know and love him would never again languish around some cesspool of despair.

Upon arriving at the pool, Jesus looked for the most hopeless sufferer; by restoring that person to wholeness, he could stir a vital hope for healing in the rest. He scanned the crowd with a slow, penetrating gaze. Sprawled on the five porches surrounding the pool were all manner of desperate people.[3] Upon seeing him, most of them brightened and stirred; perhaps they were hoping for alms or for just a warm word of encouragement and kindness.

Lost in the shadows at the back of one portico was a man who didn't stir. He didn't move or look up, though a wave of anticipation was rippling through everybody else. He just lay there inert and hopeless, waiting to die.

Jesus walked toward the man, stepping gingerly over the other sufferers, who were packed closely together. Many of them reached up, and he touched them with tenderness and kindness. But he pressed on, not to be denied his prize.

Finally reaching the man crumpled up in a ball at the back of the crowd, Jesus knelt before him. Gently he put his hand under the man's chin and raised his head. Peering into the man's hollow, darkened eyes, Jesus asked, "Do you want to be made well?" (5:6). For a moment the man stared at him blankly while the other sufferers began to murmur in discontent.

After all, at first blush it seemed a ridiculous question: "Do you want to be made well?" The man had been lying by the

---

3 The five pillars that supported these porches can still be seen today in Jerusalem at the site of Bethesda's Pool.

pool for thirty-eight years (5:5). It didn't take a rocket scientist to figure out he came there hoping for healing.

Still there was something about the man that registered his ambivalence about getting well. For it was only after Jesus observed that the man had been lying there a *long* time (5:6) that he asked, "Do you want to be made well?"

It is an important question to ponder when seeking deliverance from our own infirmities. For especially in illnesses of the mind and spirit there are often hidden gains that tend to reinforce our paralysis. And sometimes we become so accustomed to the contours of our bondage that it forms a comfortable cocoon we don't want to leave.

Our tendency to procrastinate, for example—which at one level we hate—may actually be a way of protecting ourselves. For if after procrastinating our effort is judged inadequate, we can console ourselves by saying, "Well, if only I'd had a little more time, I would have done better." A bitter, festering anger toward a parent may be a way of refusing to take responsibility for our own lives. A persistent, low-level depression may be the psyche's way of honoring our unspoken belief that we don't deserve to be happy.

Certainly these interpretations don't apply in every case. But most of the time when we are stuck—paralyzed, if you will—by Beth-zatha's Pool, it is because our condition is meeting some hidden need we have not yet recognized. Thus, the first step in healing is often identifying the unacknowledged motivations that keep us mired where we are.

"Do you want to be made well?" Jesus asks us. In all likelihood the honest answer is, "Yes, Lord, I want to be well . . . *if* you will help me conquer the fears that for so long have kept me in bondage." "Yes, Lord, I want to be well . . . *if* you will help me shoulder the added responsibilities of a more robust and able life." "Yes, Lord, I want to be well . . . *if* you will cast out the demon that keeps telling me I don't deserve any better than this."

"Yes, Lord, I want to be well *if* . . ." If what?

In asking for healing, it is crucial to fill in that blank. For in doing so we identify the very fears from which we need deliverance.

From the response of the man by Beth-zatha's Pool, it is obvious that Jesus read him right. He didn't answer Jesus' question with even a qualified yes. Instead, he erupted in a depressing litany of woes and explained why for him healing wasn't possible: "Sir, I have no one to put me into the pool when the water is stirred up; and while I am making my way, someone else steps down ahead of me" (5:7).

The perpetually troubled soul tends to blame his or her woes on others. Apparently it never occurred to this man to wonder why in thirty-eight years of trying he had never summoned anyone to his aid. Might his own negative, caustic spirit have been a factor? But facing such a difficult, probing question required a measure of moral courage; it was so much easier just to blame.

The problem with blaming, even when the blaming carries some element of truth, is that it only serves to reinforce our paralysis. If someone else is responsible for my problem, then only that person can fix it, and that leaves me utterly at another's mercy! But when I begin to claim responsibility for that part of the problem or issue that is mine, I have found the leverage for change. Making whatever changes I can—even if another withholds his or her consent or cooperation—moves me in the direction of healing.

Coach John Wooten, winning UCLA basketball coach, led his team to greatness with the philosophy, "Nobody is defeated until he starts blaming somebody else. My advice is: Don't fix the blame; fix the problem."[4]

Unless, of course, you prefer keeping the problem because it has become so fused with your identity that you don't know who you are without it. And that, I'm convinced, is what happened to the paralytic by Beth-zatha's Pool: paralysis wasn't merely his condition. It was who he was. His soul had assumed the shriveled, misshapen cast of his body. If truth be told, after thirty-eight years of being frozen from the waist down, he was scared to death of learning to walk again. So he waved Jesus off with the same tired recital of excuses and blame he had used a thousand times before.

---

4 *Parables, etc.* 14, no. 10 (December 1994), 2.

That's probably where I would have taken the hint and walked away. I would have respected the man's "space" and left him to wither and die in his miserable condition. Under my breath I might have muttered, "Good riddance" as I looked for someone more deserving of my efforts.

But Jesus didn't shrug his shoulders, give up, and walk away. Instead, he knelt beside that washed up, despondent little man. Peering deep into his stone cold eyes, the Master whispered words of life: "Take my hand . . . stand up . . . and walk!"

Startled, the man reached for Jesus' hand, gingerly, as a frail nursing home resident reaches for a visitor. Jesus took the hand and gently squeezed, infusing his strength into a tortured, frightened soul. There was a hint of life in the sufferer's eyes as Jesus nodded his encouragement. Then Jesus drew him to his feet, pulling with one hand and supporting with the other. The man who had been on the ground for thirty-eight years rose unsteadily, like a newborn fawn finding its legs, until at last he stood confident and free. The milling multitude looked on in amazement as the man everyone else had given up on found hope and healing.

Now, to be sure, this healing wasn't typical of Jesus. Usually he required some evidence of faith on the part of the sufferer, some show of spunk and desire. But here Jesus came upon someone so defeated that he couldn't even claim healing when it was staring him in the face. So Jesus gave him a healing on the house—no hoops to jump through, no down payment required, no seven steps to spiritual wholeness—just a lavish, extravagant gift of grace.

It is a measure of Jesus' greatness that sometimes he bets on a loser. If he did not, I—and countless others—would still be lying by our own pools of desperation. For I've been there—haven't you?—paralyzed by foreboding and fear, utterly drained of resources and strength.

Maybe it was when clouds of depression began gathering once more and you, tired of fighting, collapsed before the storm. Or maybe it was when you learned your mother wouldn't beat the odds this time and the cancer would finally claim her life. Maybe it was when the job, marriage, or future on which you had pinned your hopes came crashing down.

There you lay, broken and defeated, by Beth-zatha's Pool. Everyone's suggestions for getting back on your feet sounded so hollow. Somehow, putting on a smiley face just couldn't pierce the depths of your darkness. Finally, people got tired of fooling with you and started stepping over you or around you, pretending not to see, leaving you utterly forsaken and all alone. It looked as if you might stay stuck there forever.

Then one day Jesus found you. He found you in a friend who walked in after everyone else walked out. He found you in the embrace of a church that not only talked about grace but made it happen. He found you in some word from the Scriptures that came alive, stepped off the page, and lodged in your heart. You looked up from your troubles and saw his hand. Gingerly you took it. With a gentle but steady tug, he pulled you to your feet. And unsteadily at first, but with more assurance day by day, you learned to walk again.

An old legend tells of a man lost in his travels who wandered into a bed of quicksand. Confucius saw the man's predicament and said, "It is evident people should stay away from places like this."

Next Buddha observed the situation and said, "Let this one's plight be a lesson to those who would not repeat his folly."

Then Muhammed came by and said to the sinking man, "Alas, it is the will of Allah."

Finally, Jesus appeared: "Take my hand, brother," said the Master, "and let me pull you out."

This is gospel! This is good news! In Jesus Christ, God has sent one who doesn't merely offer insight, but a grace sufficient to pull us to our feet and give us another chance. Sometimes people are so broken up and beaten down that insight alone can't save them. That's when they need a Savior. That's when they need the Lord of life to step into their darkness and offer his hand. Those who take it will find the strength and hope to risk trying again.

Still, even God's grace in Jesus Christ is no miracle cure. Even so potent a force as this can work no magic apart from our active participation. This I take to be the meaning of Jesus' enigmatic comment to the paralytic: "See, you have been made well! Do not sin any more, so that nothing worse happens to you" (5:14).[5] For soon, the former paralytic was lapsing into the victim script he knew so well. When asked by the religious authorities why he was carrying his bed on the Sabbath—a technical violation of the rules[6]—he resorted to blaming once again: "The man who healed me told me to do it." Then later, after learning Jesus' identity, he actually went to the authorities and squealed on him (5:15-16).

It would appear that this man's healing didn't take. Sure, he was healed of his physical infirmity, but for Jesus that was small change. The deeper healing was and is the healing of the inner person. And here—in the depths of his person—the paralytic healed by Beth-zatha's Pool stayed as locked up as ever. He refused Jesus' summons to live in God's grace, preferring his blind, blaming ways instead. And that made him the man even Jesus couldn't cure.

Physical healing is wonderful when it happens, but that's not the only kind of healing Jesus came to give. His healing of warped, twisted bodies was just the warm-up show for the main attraction: making people whole on the *inside* even when physical healing isn't possible.

An eminent plastic surgeon tells of a teenager who lost his hand in an accident. When the young man came to his office, the doctor said, "So tell me about your handicap."

The boy responded with fire in his eyes. "Sir, I don't have a handicap. I just don't have a right hand."

As the interview progressed, the doctor was astounded to learn this remarkable young man was the leading scorer on his high school football team.[7]

---

5 In John 9:3 Jesus explicitly rejected the notion that all suffering is caused by sin. In the case of the paralytic by Beth-zatha's Pool, however, it appears there was a direct correlation between the man's attitude and his plight.

6 Carrying one's bed could be construed as "work" and hence was technically forbidden on the Sabbath, a day of rest.

7 *Dynamic Illustrations*, January/February 1995, "Attitude."

Still today, Jesus Christ can bring the inner healing that begets such a gutsy, resilient spirit. He is still on the prowl by Beth-zatha's Pool looking for broken, defeated souls everyone else has written off. He's willing to take a chance on you and gift you with his life and love. With his help, you can be the person you want to be. You can shake whatever paralysis has left you immobile and hopeless to find a new beginning in his grace.

But only do it, only *dare* it, if in your heart you really want healing, because if you let Jesus Christ into your life and actively seek to follow him, things aren't going to stay the same. Hang around him long enough and healing happens.

O holy Christ, thank you for loving me
when I don't know how to love myself.
Now stir me from whatever apathy or fear
has left me paralyzed. And give me the faith
to strike after you in longing and love.
In the power of your living presence, set me free.
Amen.

Questions for Reflection

1. Is it cruel to suggest that people sometimes become so wedded to their infirmities that they don't want to give them up? Why or why not?
2. Why is a paralysis of one's own making so easy to see in others and so hard to recognize in ourselves?
3. In the garden of Eden, Adam blamed Eve for his moral lapse, and Eve blamed the serpent (Genesis 3:12-13). Why is blaming so universal in human experience?
4. Can you relate your own experience of being by Beth-zatha's Pool? In what guise did deliverance come?
5. Can you relate the warning, "Do not sin any more, so that nothing worse happens to you" (5:14), to your own experience? In the words of Hebrews 12:1-2, what is the "weight" or "sin" that hinders you in your longing to follow Christ?

CHAPTER 8

Equal to God?

John 5:16-24

In his book *Putting Out the Sacred Fires*, Elie Wiesel tells a Jewish fable about a man who approached the heavenly throne with a question. "Which is harder," he asked, "being a man or being God?"

"Why, being God," the Creator answered. "I have a universe to run—planets, galaxies, and all the rest. All you have to worry about is your family and your job."

"True enough," said the man. "But you have infinite time and power. For us the hard part is getting the job done given our limited strength and life span."

"Trust me," said God. "Being God is much harder than you think."

"Tell you what," said the man, "why don't you and I trade places for one second. Then you will know what it's like to be a man, and I'll know what it's like to be God. Just one second, that's all. Then we'll change places back again."

Reluctantly, God agreed. The man became God, and God became a man. But once on the heavenly throne, the man double-crossed his Maker and refused to surrender his divine prerogatives. And that is why—the story goes—the world is such a mess. Because ever since, man has ruled the world and God has been in exile.[1]

That legend ably explains the tragedy of the human situation apart from God's guidance and grace, for whenever men and women aspire to be God or to play God, madness multiplies and sorrows soar.

But on the issue of God taking up the mantle of our humanity, the Christian story has its own unique twist. Christians believe that when God became man in Jesus Christ, the Creator did not abdicate the throne. Rather, the eternal Son of God stepped out from eternity to indwell a human life and woo a wayward world.

Unlike the man in the fable, Jesus didn't spring from the stage of the world to orchestrate a hostile takeover of heaven. Rather, he descended from heaven as an unspeakable gift of grace. That, at least, is how John's Gospel tells the story.

The Pharisees, however, read the cards differently. They considered Jesus yet another pretender to God's throne. They recognized his brilliance, compassion, and uncanny powers, but the confident, self-assured manner in which Jesus identified his actions with God's actions left them shaking their heads and grinding their teeth. To them Jesus was a hometown boy who had grown too big for his britches.

The conflict recorded in John 5:16-24 erupts after Jesus' healing of the paralytic by Beth-zatha's Pool. The Pharisees went looking for Jesus, planning to pick a fight over his healing on the Sabbath. But in the ensuing discussion, Jesus let an observation slip that explodes like a Molotov cocktail: "Look, *my* Father works on the Sabbath, and so do I" (5:17).

The Pharisees' mouths fell open in disbelief. Did he really say what they thought he said? To equate his healings with God's providence was madness. And to speak of the awesome, glorious deity of the Old Testament with the mundane word *Father* was utter blasphemy. Yet Jesus called God "Father" with a naturalness and ease that left the Pharisees boiling with

---

[1] From Elie Wiesel, *Putting Out the Sacred Fires*, 63-64. Quoted in *Parables, etc.*, 14, no. 12 (February 1995), 4.

rage.[2] In their minds he—an ordinary mortal—was making himself equal with God.

As the conversation in John 5 unfolds, however, it is clear that Jesus did not wish to be considered equal with God, at least not as the Pharisees used the phrase. For what did he say in response to their charge? "Very truly, I tell you, the Son can do nothing on his own, but only what he sees the Father doing" (5:19).

In other words, Jesus was not setting up a rival business in hopes of stealing the old man's clients. Instead, he was evermore the loving, devoted Son. As he would later say in this very chapter of John, "I can do nothing on my own . . . because I seek to do not my own will but the will of him who sent me" (5:30). Those hardly sound like the words of someone clamoring to "get ahead."

No, Jesus didn't strut about proclaiming his equality with God. Instead, he preferred to speak of his relationship to God in terms of oneness: "The Father and I are one" (John 10:30). This was an intimate communion forged in love in which two hearts beat as one. An apt analogy might be a thriving marriage in which two people know each other so well that one partner sometimes knows what the other is thinking before a word is spoken. Jesus' oneness with God sprang from such a divine dance of love. At every turn his love for God so sculpted the contours of his life that he became a crystal clear window into eternity. When people looked at him, they didn't just see a five-foot, six-inch Jewish carpenter; they saw clear through to God.

In Rome there is a palace with a great high dome. Inside that dome is a painting known as "The Dawn" by Guido Reni. In order that visitors may see this masterpiece, a table has been placed directly beneath the dome, and on the table, a mirror.

---

2 The New Testament was written in Greek, but Jesus' native tongue was Aramaic. In that language his preferred word for God was *Abba*, a remembrance that is preserved in the New Testament (Mark 14:36; Romans 8:15; Galatians 4:6). The Aramaic *Abba* was a child's word for his or her father. "Daddy" or "Papa" is probably closer to the original than the more formal "Father."

When one peers into the mirror, one is able to see the majestic painting far above.[3]

This was the effect Jesus had on all he met: in him they saw a crystal clear image of God. He brought God near as that earthbound mirror situated beneath the dome makes Reni's painting accessible for viewing. Jesus' love for the one he called "Father"[4] was so intense and pure, he was like a mountain lake in which the grandeur of the Rockies glimmers and shines.

Now if one can sign off on such an exalted view of Jesus, hang on, for there is more: a good many people—even many non-Christians—can and do affirm that Jesus was a stunning revelation of divine glory. So, one might argue, is a particularly moving sunset, a great oratorio, or the moral courage of a Mahatma Gandhi.

In reflecting on the wonder of what God had done in Jesus Christ, the Church meant to say a great deal more. It meant to say that Jesus was not a mere reflection of divine glory. He was not yet another moon hanging in the religious heavens. Rather, he was and is the very light of God shattering our darkness. And as a sunbeam is one with the sun from which it sprang, so Jesus was and is of a piece with the God from whom he came.

In other words, something absolutely unique and unprecedented was going on in Jesus' life. And so, at the very beginning of his Gospel, John pulls back the curtain of eternity and says, "Look. Jesus isn't just a word *from* God. Jesus is the word *of* God filling out a human life." "In the beginning was the Word, and the Word was *with* God, and the Word *was* God . . . And the Word became *flesh* and lived among us" (John 1:1,14).

Thus, Jesus is God up close, the very presence and truth of the Holy snuggling up to us in a first-century carpenter from

---

3 *The Pastor's Story File* 1, no. 4 (April 1985), 3.

4 While the "Father" is Jesus' preferred word for God in the Gospel of John, that does not mean God is to be conceived of as male. "God is spirit, and those who worship [God] must worship in spirit and truth" (John 4:24). God's "fatherhood" in the teaching of Jesus encompasses both feminine and masculine traits.

Nazareth. Or in Bishop John A. T. Robinson's gripping phrase, Jesus is the human face of God.[5]

A little boy was shaken awake in his upstairs bedroom by a fearsome thunderstorm. Terrified, he dashed downstairs to his parents' bedroom. After hugging and reassuring him, the mother said, "Now go on back up to your bedroom. I'm sure God will watch over you."

Unconvinced, the little fellow shot back, "Why don't *you* go upstairs and sleep with God? I want to stay down here and sleep with daddy!"

Jesus took the awesome Sovereign of Old Testament faith out of the remotest heaven and brought God near in a presence that could cuddle a child, caress a leper, and wipe the tears from the face of a prostitute. He didn't just wax eloquent about God; he brought God near. And when Jesus walked away from some broken soul made well by his touch, that person gaped after him in bewilderment and awe. For in the hands of this Jewish carpenter, people thought they saw the fingerprints of God.

Later the Church would hammer out the doctrine of the Trinity as a way of trying to interpret Jesus' unique relationship to God. Unfortunately, that discussion generated a lot of high-flown theological language that seems remote to our lives today. But at the heart of the Church's confession of the Trinity was and is this conviction: that while Jesus the man was ever subordinate to God, by virtue of that very obedience, the eternal Word of God—or the eternal Son of God—found a ready home in Jesus of Nazareth's life. And thus, while Jesus wasn't "equal to God" in the sense the Pharisees feared—namely, in bumping God off the throne—he was equal in the sense that in his very person the living God drew near.

For me, Jesus' relationship to the one he called "Father" is rather like that of the surf to the ocean. I have long been captivated by the beauty of the sea, but as a young child, I found the depths of the ocean terrifying and overwhelming. The surf,

---

5 John A. T. Robinson, *The Human Face of God* (Philadelphia: Westminster Press, 1973).

however, was an inviting place where I could splash and play with abandon in the embrace of my big blue friend.

Perhaps we could say that Jesus Christ is the surf where we feel safe making friends with the sea. He is where we enter the vast, grand mystery of God. To be sure, God is greater than Jesus only. In the words of the Church, God is a rich communion of love involving not only the Son but also the Father and the Holy Spirit.

Yet to know the Son is to know the Father, as surely as the water splashing a toddler's knees in the surf is the very same water that is found twenty thousand leagues under the sea. For while God may be *more* than Jesus, God is not *other* than Jesus.

And thus we come to the verse in John 5 that is the great divide: "All may honor the Son just as they honor the Father. Anyone who does not honor the Son does not honor the Father who sent him" (v. 23).

"Now wait just a minute!" protest those who choke on such language. "To say that Jesus was a stirring revelation of divine glory is one thing. But to suggest he is due the very adoration and awe that belong to God alone is a shameless blasphemy! Clearly John is putting words into Jesus' mouth, for Jesus, the simple Galilean sage of the other Gospels, could never have uttered words like this!"

The truth is, however, that even in Matthew, Mark, and Luke, Jesus is hardly reserved and unassuming. Even there he speaks of God as his Father in an intimately personal way, waves aside centuries of hallowed religious tradition as though swatting at gnats, and is even so impertinent as to forgive sins—definitely not the sort of actions one would associate with a meek, mousy soul!

Just for the sake of argument, let us concede that John turned up the voltage on some of Jesus' sayings. Let us concede that everything Jesus says in John's Gospel is not a verbatim transcript but represents John's attempt to draw out the deeper meaning of Jesus' life, death, and resurrection. Does that compromise the validity of these words? Not for me! Did not Jesus promise, "I still have many things to say to you, but you cannot bear them now. When the Spirit of truth comes, he will guide you into all the truth . . . he will take what is mine and declare it to you" (John 16:12-15)? Only after the resurrection did the disciples finally recognized the staggering magnitude of their Master.

On occasion, most of us have taken another's remark or observation the wrong way. But later, after gaining additional insight or understanding, the person's words took on a whole new meaning. In an infinitely greater way, Jesus' life took on a whole new meaning in light of his Easter triumph. For the resurrection fully disclosed who Jesus was. Thus, when the Gospel writers penned their witness, they let the light of Easter shine on his person, which is not to say they misrepresented his life and ministry, but rather that they more fully drew out its meaning.

Therefore, the issue isn't whether the historical Jesus said every word attributed to him in John's Gospel. The issue is whether this Gospel provides an accurate portrait of who Jesus was and is. Each person must make his or her own decision about that. As for me, I'm forging my life on the conviction that Jesus is not some gifted sage from the long-ago and far-away. Rather, he was and is the very presence of God drawing near, who takes our haggard lives in his hands and breathes the life of God into our souls.

Why do I believe this? Because when I cling to Jesus, I find myself drawn deeper into the mystery of the sea. He doesn't lead me farther afield of God, as the Pharisees feared. Rather, to know and love him is to know and love the Father of all mercies from whom he sprung. Indeed, apart from Jesus Christ I don't even know who God is. But in and through him, God has taken a face and a name. Because of him and him alone, I know it is safe to cast myself upon the everlasting arms.

Leslie Weatherhead tells the story of an aged Scot who was quite ill, so the family's minister was called. As the clergyman entered the sick room, he noticed an empty chair drawn near the bed. "Well, Donald," said the pastor, "I see I'm not your first visitor today."

The old man looked puzzled for a moment and then noticed the empty chair as the minister nodded in its direction.

"Well, pastor, let me tell you about that chair," he said. "Many years ago I found it quite difficult to pray, so one day I shared this problem with my minister at the time. He told me not to worry so much about how to pray—what technique or posture to use. Instead, he suggested I just sit down, pull up a chair opposite me, and imagine Jesus sitting in it. Then I should talk with Jesus as I would any other friend. And that," said the Scotsman, "is what I've been doing ever since."

A few days later, the daughter of the old gentleman called the pastor. She was quite shaken, as her father had just died without giving any indication his death was imminent. "I had just gone to lie down for an hour or two," she said, "for he seemed to be resting so comfortably. When I came back, he was gone."

"It was the strangest thing," she continued. "He was just as I left him, except that now his hand was laying on that chair he always kept at his bedside."

"It's not so strange," the minister answered. "I understand."[6]

For centuries Jesus has been the unseen Friend of count- less souls who entrusted their all to him. He has calmed their fears in the face of every challenge, even when they stared into the gaping jaws of death. Still today all who cast their lot with him will be drawn ever deeper into the wonder and love of God until at last the words of the Carpenter sound as the word of God within the soul: "Anyone who hears *my* word and believes *him who sent me* has . . . passed from death to life" (5:24).

So go ahead. Take a chance on Jesus. Put a toe in the water, reach for his hand, and let him draw you ever deeper into the welcoming waves of God's presence and the unfathomable depths of God's love.

Take my hand, Lord Jesus, and lead me ever deeper
into the love and mercy of God, for it has pleased
the Father of all mercies to reach for me in you.
Amen.

---

6 *Parables, etc.,* 6, no. 4 (April 1986), 3.

Questions for Reflection

1. Jesus' preferred word for God was "Father." Some argue that that word is too full of sexist connotations to be usable in our day. Do you agree? Why or why not?
2. An early Christian hymn preserved in Philippians 2:6-11 says that Christ did not regard equality with God as something to be "exploited" (NRSV) or "grasped" (NIV). How does that passage shed light on the "equality" of the Father and Son in John 5?
3. The author of this chapter likens the union of Jesus and God to that of the surf and the ocean. Bishop John A. T. Robinson suggests Jesus is the "human face of God." What other images might you suggest?
4. How does one "honor the Son" (5:23)? Relate the phrase to both worship and discipleship.
5. In 5:24 Jesus says "Anyone who hears my word *and* believes him who sent me has eternal life." In John's Gospel believing in Jesus and believing in God are one movement of the heart. While other religions profess belief in "God" apart from Jesus, can a fully Christian faith ever separate the two?

CHAPTER 9

Hate Is Not a Family Value

John 8:1-11[1]

A man was awakened in the middle of the night by the shrill ringing of a phone. Upon answering it, he was greeted by a frantic, sobbing girl. "Daddy," she blurted out, "I'm *pregnant.*"

Though startled and confused, the groggy father managed to confess not only his disappointment, but also his concern. The next day he and his wife each wrote letters conveying both their sorrow and steadfast love.

Three days later the man and his wife received another phone call from their daughter. She confessed shock at their letters because she had never called them in the first place nor was she pregnant. Apparently some other distraught girl had phoned the wrong number. Nonetheless, the parents' letters were not wasted. They became a treasured keepsake of love. Here are some excerpts:

> Though I weep inside, I can't condemn you, because I sin too. Your transgression is no worse than mine. It's just different. . . . We're praying much. We love you more than I can say. And respect you, too, as always.

---

[1] John 8:1-11 is not found in many ancient manuscripts of John's Gospel; hence, in most modern translations it is printed in brackets (see, e.g., NRSV) and its uncertain status footnoted. However, the incident appears to be authentic to Jesus' ministry and certainly represents the spirit of his teaching and person.

Remember, God's love is in even this, maybe especially
in this. This is a day of testing, but hold our ground we
must. God will give us the victory. We're looking forward to your being at home.

Love, Dad.[2]

Forgiveness of that magnitude has transforming power. It
doesn't make light of one's offense. In fact, such forgiveness is
remarkable precisely because it recognizes the gravity of one's
offense. But when the burden of one's guilt is met by so lavish
a grace, it sets the sinner free to make a fresh start. That was
the brand of forgiveness Jesus taught and embodied.

The Pharisees, however, saw things very differently. They
were the "law and order" crowd who considered Jesus soft on
crime. In their view, assuring people of God's unconditional love
only encouraged them to sin, so they branded Jesus a dangerous heretic and did everything in their power to discredit him.

In his book *Meeting Jesus Again for the First Time*, Marcus
Borg suggests that the Pharisees' core value was *holiness*.[3] They
believed in a black and white world. Things were either good
or evil, pure or impure, righteous or unrighteous. By contrast,
Jesus' core value was *compassion*. He was quick to help and
slow to condemn—not because he was soft on sin, but because
he recognized sin as a far more sinister force than the Pharisees
imagined. It was not like dirt that could simply be wiped clean.
It was more like an infection that had to be cured from deep
within.

The story of the woman caught in adultery shows the collision of Jesus' core value of compassion with the Pharisees'
core value of holiness. The episode began as Jesus was teaching in the temple (8:2). Suddenly the Pharisees burst in and
hurled a sobbing woman before him. Red hot with indignation,
they announced their indictment for all to hear: the woman

---

2 *In Other Words*, 5, no. 1 (January/February 1995), 5. From *Moody Monthly*, September 1991, 6.
3 Marcus J. Borg, *Meeting Jesus Again for the First Time: The Historical Jesus and the
   Heart of Contemporary Faith* (San Francisco: HarperSanFrancisco, 1995), 46ff.

was caught in the very act of committing adultery (8:4). As the crowd milling about Jesus shrank back in shock and shame, the Pharisees demanded the Teacher's verdict. Would he join them in condemning her? Surely not even he could defend so notorious a sinner!

The Pharisees stood glaring while the woman, scantily clad, trembled and shook like a reed in the wind. The gang leader, sensing victory, tapped his foot impatiently. Then, just when it seemed they had the young rabbi trapped, Jesus stooped and began doodling in the temple's earthen courtyard. The mouths of the Pharisees fell open in surprise. They shot looks of disbelief at one another that said, "Can you believe this guy?" Meanwhile, unperturbed, Jesus' doodled at their feet.

Some argue that Jesus was up to something far more exalted than mere doodling. They say, for example, that he began writing the sins of the Pharisees. In the dirt he listed, one by one, their own moral failures. But if that were the case, it seems odd they kept pressing him for a response. Given that scenario, they probably would have slipped away then rather than later (8:9). No, in all probability Jesus just doodled in the dust making shapes and curlicues as a way of gaining time and gathering his wits.

To be sure, Jesus was incensed that the Pharisees had no concern or compassion for this woman. She was just a pawn in their game of tripping him up. And the hypocrisy of their self-righteous condemnation was appalling. Where, for example, was the man involved in the adulterous act?[4]

Had Jesus let his anger run away with him, he would have played right into their hands. By instinctively leaping to the woman's defense, it might appear he was indifferent to the law of God as his critics charged. So Jesus stalled, bought himself a little time, and pondered what to do.

The Pharisees, however, sensing the kill, would not be denied. They kept pestering Jesus with questions, even as he doodled at their feet. Finally, he stood erect. When he rose,

---

[4] According to the law of Moses, both the man and the woman caught in adultery faced stoning. See Leviticus 20:10; Deuteronomy 22:23-24.

he had a rock the size of a baseball in his hand. Thrusting it in the face of the Pharisees' ringleader, he spit out the challenge: "Let anyone among you who is without sin be the first to throw a stone at her" (8:7). Then he grabbed the Pharisee's wrist, twisted his arm, and forced the rock into his palm. And before the baffled gaze of all, Jesus squatted once more and began doodling again (8:8).

There was a deathly silence as everyone waited to see what would happen. The Pharisee with the rock in his hand looked from Jesus to the terrified woman and then at his feet. There his eyes stayed locked as despite himself Jesus' indictment rang in his ears and unsettled his heart. Finally, he dropped the rock, and it landed with a thud on the ground. The woman shuddered, thinking the rain of stones had begun. But instead, the Pharisee turned and walked away, no longer disgusted with her, but with himself. Then as the others saw their leader withdraw from the fray, Jesus' challenge came home to each of them in turn. They also began to slink away, one by one, until at last only Jesus and the woman remained.

Once more Jesus straightened up. Putting his robe about the trembling woman, Jesus asked her, "Woman, where are they? Has no one condemned you?" (8:10).

Shaking her head in disbelief, she answered, "No one, sir."

Jesus lifted her chin with his finger and looked straight into her eyes. "Neither do I condemn you. Go your way, and from now on do not sin again" (8:11).

In this encounter we see Jesus diffusing a volatile situation with his matchless wit. With those immortal words—"Let anyone among you who is without sin be the first to throw a stone at her"—he created a classic double bind. On the one hand, he gave the Pharisees permission to stone the woman. After all, according to the law of Moses, such a penalty was permitted. But Jesus argued that they were free to administer such justice only if they themselves were without sin. That was the hook that caught the Pharisees up short and silenced their proud, judgmental spirit.

Granted, the Pharisees probably were not guilty of overt adultery. Their emphasis on observing the letter of the law made that unlikely. But in the Sermon on the Mount, Jesus charged that merely looking at another with lust constituted "committing adultery in the heart" (Matthew 5:28). It was in highlighting such "crimes of the heart"—and not merely one's outward, public failings—that Jesus turned the tables on the Pharisees, for he stood in the prophetic tradition that held that while others judge by outward appearances, God looks on the heart (1 Samuel 16:7).

When the Exxon *Valdez* spilled its oil in Alaska's Prince William Sound, the nation looked on in horror. What few realized, however, was that the *Valdez* disaster paled in comparison to the environmental disaster unleashed every year by unwitting consumers. American "do-it-yourselfers" annually dump 193 million gallons of motor oil in storm drains, trash receptacles, and back alleys. That's twenty times the amount spilled in Alaska in 1989.[5]

When someone commits a sin of epic proportions like the woman caught in adultery, the Pharisee in us shrieks in horror. But so often we are blind to the sum total of our self-perceived "little sins" that nonetheless loom large in the eyes of God. The enduring appeal of Phariseeism is that it rigs the game in such a way that others' sins are exposed while ours are ignored. This is possible only because Phariseeism focuses on the *Valdez*-type sins that everyone can see. Thus, the confirmed adulterer or flagrant homosexual is considered a choice target for our righteous indignation. Indeed, the growth of some religious institutions in our day is fueled by the fanning of hatred toward liberal politicians, homosexuals, and doctors who perform abortions.

But our Lord's charge—"Let anyone among you who is without sin be the first to throw a stone at her"—should sound the death knell to every religious crusade that attacks another's alleged sins while remaining blissfully blind to one's own. For if Jesus' endless tangling with the Pharisees is any indication, there was nothing he so deplored as a self-righteous piosity. Nothing is so foreign to his spirit as the gleeful denunciation of those who have lost their way. Those who in the name of

---

5 *INC.* 13, no. 8 (August 1991), 44.

Jesus Christ express contempt for sinners do not speak for the Master. As a recently spotted bumper sticker would remind us, "Hate Is *Not* a Family Value."

Along with Jesus' pointed challenge to the Pharisees we must not forget his challenge to the woman. Jesus saved her from the Pharisees not to gloss over her sin, but that he might set her free. His charge to her was clear and commanding: "Go your way, and from now on do not sin again" (8:11).

Those words are as crucial to the story as the phrase more often quoted about not casting the first stone. But we seriously misread both the story and Jesus if we emphasize his condemnation of Phariseeism while muting his invitation to life: "Go and sin no more." Jesus didn't come to minimize the reality of sin; he came to wrest people free of its power.

Take, for example, his teaching about lust: "Everyone who looks at a woman with lust has already committed adultery with her in his heart" (Matthew 5:28). But that is not to say that committing "adultery in the heart" is as damaging as acting out the impulse. "Adultery in the heart" is a sin against oneself and God. Actual adultery compounds the injury by involving others.

I'm reminded of the time Jimmy Carter was asked by a interviewer from *Playboy* if he had ever lusted. When he answered truthfully, "Yes," he plunged fifteen points in the polls. Some twenty years later on the *Jay Leno Show*, Carter recalled an incident that happened while on a book-signing tour. An attractive young woman sidled up to him and said, "If you still have lust in your heart, I'm available."[6] Fortunately, Jimmy Carter was quicker to confess his lustful impulses than to act on them. Thus, the corrosive effects of his lust were contained within himself.

Jesus' comment, "Let anyone among you who is without sin be the first to throw a stone," was uttered as a rejection of judgmentalism, of looking down on others. It should not be misconstrued to mean moral distinctions do not matter. For the

---

6 Ann S. Wright, *Move Over, Goldfish: The Secrets to Surviving in the Parsonage* (Greensboro, N.C.: Teco Printing Co., n.d.), p. 33.

first comment—"Let anyone among you who is without sin be the first to throw a stone"—must ever be held in tension with the second—"Go and sin no more."

Had the woman caught in adultery offered some slick rationalization to justify her immorality, Jesus would have rejected it out of hand. But no such rationalization was offered. Standing before one who radiated the purity of divine love, the weight of her guilt came crashing down. Suddenly she hated the shameful spectacle she had made of herself and despised the affair that had cheapened her so. In some ways the hail of rocks she had expected would have been easier to bear than the gentle force of Jesus' presence. But instead he shielded her from the Pharisees' hatred that she might be reborn by his love.

I have sometimes stood where she stood, feeling God-forsaken and all alone. Given some personal failure or folly, my internal Pharisees hauled me before Jesus, loudly denouncing my inadequacy and shame. And I was all too ready to join in the spectacle of self-condemnation. Yet there stood Jesus, regal and tall, amid the ring of angry accusers clamoring for justice. The sheen of his light drove the Pharisees back like rats fleeing the dawn until finally only he and I remained. He beckoned me near and covered the nakedness of my need with his love. Then the words of blessing sounded: "Your accusers have fled. Neither do I condemn you. Now go and sin no more."

Jesus can offer so lavish a forgiveness because at Golgotha he earned the right to give it. For in due time the defenders of the law would condemn him also. Only this time there would be no one to make his defense, no one to hold the forces of religious fanaticism at bay. Thus, he died a condemned sinner on a Roman gallows even though he was without sin. There he fulfilled the just requirements of the law, paying the penalty decreed for the woman caught in the adultery and all the rest of us sinners. Now, having borne our guilt and condemnation,[7] he offers forgiveness and new life to all who believe.

---

[7] "He was wounded for our transgressions, crushed for our iniquities; . . . and the LORD has laid on him the iniquity of us all" (Isaiah 53:5-6).

A man named Ed Barkley was aboard a train leaving Victoria Station in England. In the seat across from Barkley, a fellow passenger had a terrible seizure. As he fell to the floor, the man's traveling companion quickly knelt beside him, put his coat under the man's convulsing head, and cradled him until calmness returned. Seeing Barkley looking on in astonishment, the man cradling his friend explained, "Mister, this happens two or three times a day without warning. That's why I stay with him all the time. You see, we were buddies in Vietnam. One day I got shot up pretty bad. We were deep in the jungle, and the helicopter never came. My friend here put me on his back and carried me through the jungle for three days, snipers shooting at us all the time. Finally, he got me to safety.

"So four years ago, when I heard about his condition, I pulled up stakes and came here to be with him. Sure, it's hard sometimes, but after what he did for me, there ain't nothing I wouldn't do for him."[8]

From such a wellspring of devotion flows the believer's life also. For after what Jesus Christ did for us, is there anything we wouldn't do for him? Ironically, the just requirement of the law is fulfilled not by Pharisees who live out of a self-styled holiness, but by believers who live out of Jesus' grace. From the word of grace—"Neither do I condemn you"—spring the words of life "Go and sin no more."

So whether you're a Pharisee, a notorious sinner, or more likely, situated somewhere in between, Jesus Christ can set you free. As John wrote in the prologue of his Gospel, "The law indeed was given through Moses; grace and truth came through Jesus Christ" (1:17). He is the place where God's truth and God's grace meet and healing happens. Go to him whether you are mired in self-righteousness or self-condemnation. Forsake the glare of the Pharisee—whether your own or another's—to live in the soft light of Jesus' love.

---

8 *Proclaim*, January–March 1995, 43.

Forgive us, Lord, our razor-sharp vision
for the sins of others while remaining blind
to our own. Draw us into the circle
of your light and love so that we can see ourselves aright.
Then by the power of your life-giving grace set us free.
Amen.

Questions for Reflection

1. What do you think Jesus wrote in the dirt at the feet of the woman's accusers? The first time (8:6) and the second (8:8)?
2. Why did the Pharisees' lynch mob disperse "beginning with the elders" (8:9)? Why were the older members in the group the first to leave, and the young, the last?
3. A coworker is charged with milking the company of funds. What is the difference in being judgmental and making needed moral judgments?
4. Were the Pharisees justified in their concern that Jesus' lavish grace might encourage moral license? How does Romans 6:1-4 speak to that question?
5. How does this story shed light on Jesus' saying in Matthew 5:20: "I tell you, unless your righteousness exceeds that of the scribes and Pharisees, you will never enter the kingdom of heaven"? From where does that kind of righteousness come?

CHAPTER 10

Seeing the Light

John 9:1-41

He hated that spot by the temple gate. But in his business there was none better. Beggars can't be choosers, they say, so he swallowed the resentment that turned to fire in his stomach and kept going back.

Blind from birth, he was always Exhibit A as the proud worshipers marched by. They looked down on him with both pity and contempt. While their sins were small enough to be forgiven, his were considered beyond the pale of God's mercy. Why else would he have suffered such a terrible fate—blindness from birth—unless either he or his parents were guilty of unspeakable sin? Still, a man had to eat, so he held his cup up as the righteous walked by, hoping to hear the rattle of some jerk's pocket change.

One day as he sat stewing in his rage, he heard a band of would-be rabbis passing by. Those roving theological schools were the worst, for he always became an object lesson in a discussion of the judgment of God. As usual, one of the eager students popped the question: "Rabbi, who sinned, this man or his parents, that he was born blind?" (9:2). The blind man gritted his teeth anticipating the usual litany of condemnation and blame.

Instead, he heard startling, revolutionary words (9:3): "Nobody *sinned*," said the teacher. "This man's blindness is but the dark stage where the glory of God is about to shine."

The blind man couldn't believe his ears. There was a loud

silence as the teacher's followers also tried to absorb his words. Then in the quietness, the blind man heard soft footfalls coming his way. Instinctively, he tensed up, fearing the kicking and prodding he sometimes endured. Instead, the stranger who had just spoken drew so near that the blind man could feel the warmth of his breath. "How would you like to leave your darkness behind," whispered the unseen presence, "and step into the light of the world?"

Suddenly the man's fears receded and a ray of hope burst into his darkness. For some reason he trusted this man. He trusted the goodness that radiated from him like the warmth of the sun. Though speechless, he nodded eagerly and put all his faith in a man he couldn't see. Then he waited eagerly and expectantly for the world's light to shatter his darkness.

Only it didn't. Instead of healing, he was given an eyeful of muddy paste and was told to wash it out in Siloam's Pool (9:6-7). Instantly a sinking feeling hit his stomach. Other would-be healers had rubbed mud in his eyes, but it never made any difference.[1]

Feeling his doubt, Jesus said to him, "It's all right. Just go to the Pool of Siloam and wash your eyes." Then helping the man to his feet, Jesus pointed him in the right direction. A gentle breeze nudged him on, and the man decided to take a chance on Jesus.

Blindly groping through the streets, making a perfect spectacle of himself, the man at last reached Siloam's Pool. Kneeling before it, he cupped his hands and splashed water in his face. Then he wiped the mud from his eyes and pried his eyelids open. Suddenly light exploded in his brain. His eyes stung from the shock, and things were blurry for several seconds. But after blinking repeatedly, a little boy playing with a wooden boat came into focus on the far side of the pool. The little boy was staring at him, and the man stared back, gaping in wonder at the beauty of a child. Then his face broke into a huge smile, and with a steadiness born of sight, he rose to his feet. For the first time in his life he stood tall, strong, and unafraid.

---

[1] In the ancient world a healer's saliva was thought to have medicinal value.

Sooner or later most of us find ourselves sitting in some God-forsaken darkness. Perhaps like the blind man, we feel we are damaged goods. Because of some defect, real or imagined, others have turned their backs or looked away, and we feel all alone.

It might be the darkness of an addiction that, try as we might, we are powerless to shake. Or maybe it is the darkness of divorce, and a multitude of unanswered questions loom over us like a forest of redwoods. Maybe it is the darkness of some guilt or shame that presses in upon us with almost physical force. But in a multitude of guises, the darkness of some great despair or devastation sooner or later envelopes us all.

To make matters worse, there are always those quick to assign blame. "So who sinned, anyway—this person or his parents—that he was born blind?" Is the darkness of our own making, or can we blame Mom and Dad for one more mishap or misfortune? In the final analysis, who can say for certain, and does it matter? For while deciding whom to blame may be emotionally gratifying, it rarely if ever brings deliverance.

At last, stranded in the dark, we catch wind of Jesus. Maybe we see his name emblazoned on a bumper sticker or tacky roadside sign. Or maybe we catch a few words about him after pressing "scan" on the car radio. We would like to believe he can deliver us, as people say. But who knows? It sounds like a long shot. And how would one know where to begin?

There is the Church, of course, where one might hope to learn more about Jesus. But people say it is filled with hypocrites, and besides, the Church asks new believers to be washed in the waters of baptism. That's about as ridiculous as sending a blind man staggering through the streets of Jerusalem to wash in Siloam's Pool. Why play the fool staggering after some wild, improbable hope of healing?

Still, occasionally people get so fed up with the darkness that they take a chance on Jesus. Feeling they have nothing to lose, they call out to him, acting as if he is real even though some say he is not. Tired of playing the blame game, stuck too long in the paralysis of analysis, they ask Jesus to set them free.

Weary of the darkness, they plead for the Light of the World.

At first there may be no staggering light, just an inkling of hope born in the heart, a sense of an unseen presence, the courage to keep trying. But day by day, step by fitful step, the confidence grows that they are no longer alone but are upheld by holy love. In time they discover that trusting, loving, and following Jesus makes a radical difference in how they see themselves and the world—not a small, incremental difference like taking a new drug or trying a new diet, but a difference so phenomenal that it is like seeing one's first sunrise after thirty years in the dark.

Every year at the North Pole there are three months of total darkness. For three, solid months one never sees the sun. A man named Rudd described what that was like: "I ached and hungered to see the dawn."

Early one February morning Rudd climbed atop a windswept ridge and sat quietly facing east. When he arrived the sky was a sheet of gray. Then it became a deepening pale blue. Mountain peaks on the horizon turned purple, then crimson, then gold. There was a silent rush of color as the sun rose. Rudd stood blinking with frozen tears on his cheeks.[2]

Sometimes, before appreciating the grandeur of light, one must spend a long time in the dark. Even so, it is impossible to fathom the devotion Christians feel for their Savior until one has been set free by his light. If you've ever found yourself in a darkness so thick, so impenetrable, you thought you'd die there—and then the light of Jesus Christ led you out—you'll be forevermore bound to him. Try as you might, you'll never shake his magic from your soul.

That was certainly true of the man born blind. Once Jesus completely changed his life, everyone tried to convince the man the change wasn't for real, or for keeps, or that Jesus had nothing to do with it. But despite pressures to distance himself from this unorthodox teacher, the man born blind clung to Jesus with ruthless determination. Conditioned all his life to keep his head down and his mouth shut, he kept looking his accusers in the

---

2 *Pulpit Resource* 7, no. 3 (October-December, 1979).

eye and speaking the truth. He had been blind too long to pretend he couldn't see.

In a quick succession of scenes, John show us this man's emerging faith and courage. At first his neighbors doubt his identity. "This can't be ole Joe we used to see groveling down at the temple. This guy looks the same, but he acts so different." Hearing the chatter, the man born blind steps forward to confess, "I *am* the man!" Then he tells how Jesus opened his eyes (9:10-11).

Next, the Pharisees haul the man in. They're upset because his healing occurred on the sabbath, a technical violation of the laws governing sabbath observance. They denounce Jesus as a sinner and try to shake the man from his story. "What do *you* think of him?" they ask. "It was *your* eyes he opened." The man gives voice to the faith growing ever larger in his soul: "He is a prophet" (9:17).

Dismissing him, the Pharisees call in the man's parents. The authorities don't buy this bogus story of his being blind from birth. The parents, however, confirm that he was. "Then *you* tell us how he was healed," the Pharisees demand, their frustration mounting (9:18-19).

The parents play it safe, refusing to get involved. "He's old enough to speak for himself," they say. "Ask *him*." Clearly the man born blind got none of his newfound courage from them.

Next, the Pharisees bring the man back for further questioning. They make him swear to tell the truth, the whole truth, and nothing but the truth.[3] They're even careful to tell him the answer they want to hear. All he needs to do is denounce Jesus as a sinner. Then he can enjoy both his healing and the sanction of his culture. "We *know* that this man is a sinner," the experts announce with one accord (9:24).

But the only "expert testimony" this man is inclined to trust is his own. Standing his ground, he answers, "Whether he is a sinner, you decide. I only know that once I was blind, but now I see!" (9:25).

---

[3] "Give glory to God!" (9:24) was a technical phrase imploring one to tell the truth.

The Pharisees shake their heads and roll their eyes. Clearly they are dealing with a dimwit who must be patiently helped along. They ask him to recite the details of his healing yet again. But the man born blind has had enough. He is tired of their endless grilling and their unwillingness to accept the truth. "Why do you want to hear it all again?" he asks, with thinly veiled sarcasm. "Do you also want to become his disciples?" (9:27).

At that, the Pharisees explode in righteous indignation. "We are Moses' disciples!" they snarl. "But as for this man Jesus, we know nothing about him!"

"Well now ain't that somethin'?" says the man born blind, playing the dumb cluck they believe him to be. "You claim to know everything. Yet here someone healed a man blind from birth—something that's never happened before—and you don't have a clue about what's going on" (9:30).

At that, the Pharisees fire anxious, furtive glances all around.

"You keep trying to convince me that this Jesus is a sinner. Well, forgive me, fellas, but I don't get it. You people have told me all my life that God doesn't listen to sinners. That's why I sat outside your temple all those years dying in despair.

"But now finally something good happens to me—this Jesus heals my blindness—and you want to change the rules! Sorry, but I'm not buying. If he weren't from God, he couldn't do a thing!" (9:33).

At that, the Pharisees shoot forward in their seats, their backs arched and faces livid. The head man renders their judgment, his jaw quivering with rage: "You good-for-nothing scum! Who do you think you are? You were born in sin, and you would teach us?" And at that, they threw him out (9:34).

Suddenly the man born blind is a nobody once more. His neighbors are gossiping about him, his parents are keeping their distance, and the religious establishment has labeled him an infidel and a fool. Even his vocation as a professional beggar is gone. He is not welcome at home, in the neighborhood, at work, or even at "church." In some ways, his life has gone from bad to worse because of a man he has never seen and doesn't know where to find!

But Jesus, knowing of the man's bewilderment and pain, seeks him out: "Jesus heard that they had driven him out, and . . . he found him" (9:35). As microbiologist George Fearnehowgh once observed, "Jesus is the light of the world. And the most remarkable thing about light is the speed of its coming."

Even so, Jesus quickly finds the man without another friend in the world. "Do you believe in the Son of Man?" Jesus asks (9:35).

"And who is he, sir? Tell me, so that I may believe in him" (9:36).

Jesus answered, "You have seen him, and the one speaking with you is he" (9:37).

The once blind man responded, "Lord, I believe" (9:38). Then he knelt at Jesus' feet and offered praise and thanksgiving.

Here is the climax of the story in which the man comes to see that Jesus is not merely a gifted healer or insightful prophet, but one in whom God is uniquely, decisively present. Indeed, nothing short of the confession that Jesus is Lord will do justice to the magnitude of his person. The man first experienced Jesus as a most remarkable "man" (9:11), then as a "prophet" (9:17), then as a man from God (9:33). But his spiritual vision continued to deepen until at last he grasped the fuller glory of his newfound Master. Finally, only one word could make sense of his life-transforming experience with Jesus "'*Lord*, I believe.' And he worshiped him" (9:38).

Thus, we learn that the fullest illumination of who Jesus is not given at the beginning. As with the man born blind, our apprehension grows as we cling to Jesus in faith and devotion.

As a Baptist pastor, I am sometimes asked at what age a child is old enough to be baptized and join the church. Parents are often worried that their child doesn't know "enough" to be a committed follower of Christ. But what is "enough"? And can one ever know enough about what it means to follow Jesus?

I have only one answer to the question, "When is a child old enough to proclaim Jesus Christ as his or her Lord and Savior?" One is old enough when one has enough of a self to give it away and knows enough of Jesus to give it to him. E. Stanley Jones was asked by an eight-year-old girl, "What does it take to become a Christian?" "Darling," the great missionary reportedly answered, "it takes *you*."

Granted, such a child doesn't understand the full meaning of her confession. Neither do I. Fortunately, full understanding is not required—only the willingness to follow Jesus with whatever light one has, knowing that his radiance grows brighter with each step of the journey.

Most people want to "see the light" and be sure of their footing before committing themselves to Christ. But as the experience of the man born blind would teach us, most often the reverse is true. It is only as we dare to take a chance on Jesus—and follow him with whatever little faith we have—that his glory begins to shine. And in the crucible of our own experience, the stunning claim rings true, "I am the light of the world. Whoever follows me will never again walk in darkness but will have the light of life" (8:12).

No matter how thick the darkness, no matter how hopeless your plight, dare to whisper the Master's name. And in the soft glow of faith's dawning, take your first trembling step into the fuller light of day.

Lord Jesus, amid the darkness, I cry to you.
I have cried to everyone else, and still I sit here
hopeless and afraid. Come to me, I pray you,
in the radiance of your grace. Give me the light
I need to find my way. More than that,
be the light I need to find abundant and eternal life.
Amen.

Questions for Reflection

1. How is this healing similar and how is it different from the healing of the paralytic in John 5?
2. In this story Jesus shifts the focus from blame—"Who sinned?"—to new beginnings—"That God's works might be revealed in him." But when might clarifying blame be an appropriate step in finding healing?

3. After his healing, the man born blind was hardly recognizable to those who knew him before (9:9). What does this suggest about the nature of Christian conversion?
4. In coming to faith in Christ, the man born blind saw Jesus first as a "man" (9:11), then a "prophet" (9:17), "a man from God" (9:33), and finally as the "Lord" (9:38). Do most believers go through such a progression? Where do you find yourself on this spectrum of responses to Jesus?
5. If faith is always growing and changing, what constitutes "enough" faith to be a Christian?
6. How has your understanding of the confession, "Jesus is Lord," changed with the years?

CHAPTER 11

The Agonizing Absence

John 11:1-44

The story of Lazarus is best known for its sensational climax—Jesus prying his beloved friend from the clammy hands of death. The tale begins, however, with an experience far more typical of the life of faith, one in which we often find ourselves—confronting the agonizing *absence* of God.

Lazarus was one of Jesus' closest friends. He lived in Bethany, just two miles from Jerusalem. Whenever Jesus and the disciples were passing through, they always bedded down at Lazarus's place. Lazarus's two sisters, Mary and Martha, also loved Jesus. It was their special joy to dote on Jesus and the boys whenever the gang happened by looking for hot coffee and a soft bed.

So naturally, when Lazarus fell gravely ill, the sisters sent word to Jesus. They knew he would come as soon as he heard. Surely the one who healed strangers right and left would be at *their* place in a flash. Only he wasn't. He didn't come when they first called him and needed him most. In fact, the account says explicitly that "after having heard that Lazarus was ill, [Jesus] *stayed two days longer* in the place where he was" (11:6). Anticipating the reader's outrage, John is quick to add, "Jesus loved Martha and her sister and Lazarus." But we are left to wonder, *What kind of love is this that fails us when we need it most?*

Have you ever found yourself facing the illness of a loved one or some other terrifying trial and sent word to Jesus, beseeching his aid? If so, then maybe you were one of the lucky ones, and he showed up right away. Maybe you were delivered from a nearly fatal illness or you walked away from a car crushed in an accident in awe that your life was spared. But sooner or later the time comes when we send word to Jesus that we need him desperately, and we need him now, but he doesn't show. What are we to do then, when our loved one dies because Jesus spent too long dawdling at the edge of the universe? How can we ever love or trust him again after that?

Imagine the bitterness Mary and Martha felt when Jesus finally arrived, too little, too late. Indeed, Mary, the more delicate of the two, couldn't even bring herself to go and meet him. She stayed in the house crumpled in pain while Martha pulled herself together to do what had to be done. But when Martha confronted Jesus on the front porch, there was fire in her eyes. "Lord," she said in a voice trembling with anger, "if you had been here, my brother would not have died" (11:21). It was both an affirmation and an accusal. For mingled with the confidence that Jesus could have saved her brother was the crushing realization he had not.

This is a shock and sorrow unique to persons of faith. Those who never expected anything from God aren't left to wonder why God turned a deaf ear to their prayers. But for those who profess faith in Christ, the mourners by Lazarus' grave raise a haunting question: "Could not the one who gave sight to the blind, have saved Lazarus—or our loved one or friend?" Shouldn't the fact that we welcomed Christ into our hearts, offering him hospitality and haven, count for something when the chips are down? So why is it that sometimes when we desperately need our Lord—and he knows it because we sent word time and time again—we are confronted nonetheless with the agonizing absence of God?

The text of John's Gospel takes a stab at answering that question. Jesus interprets his delay by saying, "This illness…is for God's glory, so that the Son of God may be glorified through it" (11:4). Then later he tells his disciples, "Lazarus is dead. And for your sake I am glad that I was not there, so that you may believe" (11:14-15).

"Believe what?" we are quick to ask. Just what exactly are we supposed to believe about this one who lets us down when we need him most?

Yet Jesus seems to be saying that God's highest priority is not delivering us from pain or peril. Much to our dismay, we learn that the God who confronts us in Jesus Christ is more concerned about our spiritual maturation than our emotional comfort. And apparently there are depths of God's love we cannot know until we have met him at the edge of some unanswered prayer or unmet need.

Every farmer and gardener knows that hard, packed soil can receive no moisture. Only soil that has been broken, turned, and crumbled can be saturated with water, which in turn, promotes the growth of the seeds within it.

Perhaps so long as our lives are tightly packed and rigidly defended, God's living presence cannot unfold and grow within us. But when life levels a blow that breaks us open and maybe breaks us apart, we are able to receive God's mercies in the depths of our being.

That is not to say that God *sends* pain and suffering. But maybe God *permits* pain and suffering, knowing that the gift of God's fuller presence can only be given in seasons of struggle and desperation.[1] Indeed, the very miracles we crave may deny us the opportunity to grow into persons of compassion and grace. For such capacities cannot flower until one is "acquainted with grief." As Douglas John Hall has written, "God's problem is not that God is *not able* to do certain things. God's problem is that God loves. And love complicates the life of God as it complicates every life."[2]

After encountering Martha and hearing her bruising accusation, Jesus asked to see Mary also. At that, Mary dabbed her

---

[1] The book of Job is an extended theological treatise of this theme: God permits rather than sends Job's sufferings. As a result, Job comes to know and love God in a radically new way: "I had heard of you by the hearing of the ear, but now my eye *sees* you" (Job 42:5).

[2] Douglas John Hall, *God and Human Suffering* (Minneapolis: Augsburg, 1986), 156, quoted in Philip Yancey, *Disappointment with God: Three Questions No One Asks Aloud* (Grand Rapids: Zondervan, 1988), 71.

eyes, stuffed some extra tissues in her pockets, and went to see Jesus. But at the sight of him, she lost her composure and collapsed at his feet. Then, through her sobbing, she leveled the same charge as had her sister before her: "Lord, if you had been here, my brother would not have died" (11:32).

When Jesus saw this dear woman at his feet, devastated by sorrow, he shuddered. Or as the King James poignantly translates, "He *groaned* in the spirit" (11:33). Fighting back tears, he asked to see Lazarus' tomb.

Together, they went to the tomb. Upon seeing the place where his beloved friend lay, and seeing the shattering impact that death was having on the people he held dearest, Jesus could hold his anguish in no longer. The Lord of life put his face in his hands. His great shoulders began to heave. And Jesus wept (11:35).

Suddenly we understand. Suddenly we see that God is not untouched by our pain. Rather, the seeming delays and refusals to do our bidding are even more costly to God than to us. For the God who draws near in Jesus Christ is a loving God who cares passionately for God's children. So when for reasons hidden in the mystery of divine providence God cannot do as we beg and plead, the first tear to fall falls upon the face of God.

That the great, awesome God who flung the stars into deepest space also meets us at the place of our brokenness and pain is one of Christianity's most stunning claims. In virtually every other religion, God is viewed as a power aloof and untouchable, reigning in regal majesty above and beyond the travails of this mortal world. Christians alone believe that in Jesus Christ, God so fully entered the human drama that God knows the contours of the broken heart. Is it any wonder then that when Christians gather by the grave of a loved one, they sometimes sense the presence of the Master not observing in detachment, but coming to make for *their* loved one—as for Lazarus—an offering of tears?

In his spiritual autobiography *Now and Then*, novelist and preacher Frederick Buechner writes of teaching comparative religion at an Ivy League boys' school in the East. His students were some of the best and brightest of their generation, reveling in the freedom of inquiry that was the hallmark of their studies. But lest the budding scholars in his charge settle too quickly for the glib assumption that all great religions are saying the same thing, Buechner invited them to put Christ and Buddha side by side.

Buddha, says Buechner, sits in the lotus position. "His lips are faintly parted in the smile of one who has passed beyond every power in earth or heaven to touch him. 'He who loves fifty has fifty woes, he who loves ten has ten woes, he who loves none has no woes,' he has said. His eyes are closed."

By contrast, Christ stands in the Garden of Gethsemane, his posture slumped from the weight of the world on his shoulders. "His face is lost in shadows so that you can't even see his lips, and before all the powers in earth or heaven he is powerless. 'This is my commandment, that you love one another as I have loved you,' he has said. His eyes are also closed."

In lyric prose, Buechner presses his point home:

> The difference seems to me this. The suffering that Buddha's eyes close out is the suffering of the world that Christ's eyes close in and hallow. It is an extraordinary difference, and even in a bare classroom in Exeter, New Hampshire, I think it was as apparent to everyone as it was to me that before you're done, you have to make a crucial and extraordinary choice.[3]

The Christian faith proclaims that even when God is absent in power, God is always present in love—and not with a stern, withholding love, coldly dispensing what our Maker deems best, but with a fragile, broken love that crawls up on a cross and dies *for* us and *with* us, so that no one ever again has to die alone. Thus, even when Jesus is absent as the wonder worker we pine for, he is present as the Comforter, enabling us to endure what for now cannot be vanquished.[4] Calmed by his

---

3 Frederick Buechner, *Now and Then* (San Francisco: Harper & Row, 1983), 53-54.
4 A theme explored more fully in John 14:16ff.

grace and moved by his tears, we find the strength to choose life, even in the face of death.

This is in part the meaning of the promise: "I am the resurrection and the life. Those who believe in me, even though they die, will live, and everyone who lives and believes in me will never die" (11:25-26). On the one hand, we are given the assurance that those lost to us are awakened to new life with God: "Those who believe in me, even though they die, will live." Yet Jesus also promises that while the final resurrection must await God's future, we can still, in the face of every crushing grief and sorrow, experience some sort of resurrection now. "And everyone who lives and believes in me will *never die.*"

I know. It doesn't seem quite fair, and maybe it isn't. Despite sharing our feelings of abandonment, bewilderment, and pain, in the end, Mary and Martha got their loved one back. At the sound of Jesus' command, Lazarus stumbled from his tomb like a bear leaving its cave after a winter's hibernation. We, by contrast, are left with Jesus' presence only, while the ache of losing a loved one still burns a hole in our hearts.

But the raising of Lazarus is not meant as a sign of what we can expect from God within time. It is a sign of what is unfolding in eternity. Beyond our awareness, in a world we don't yet have eyes to see, Jesus' cry yet robs death of its prey: "Lazarus, Lynn, Harry, Helen, . . . come out!" And on the far side of that tomb where we lay them, those lost to us hear the shout of the Master. And with hearts trembling in love and awe, they stumble from the cave of death to fall into the arms of God.

Meanwhile, we're called to experience those little resurrections that mirror the great resurrection yet to be. "He or she who believes in me shall never die." A killing grief begins to lift, and our first laugh tumbles out. A despair we thought would destroy our faith serves to steel and deepen it. Out of our very brokenness and pain a more robust and vital selfhood begins to grow. Lying in some tomb of doubt and disbelief, we feel faith, hope, and love beginning to stir to life within us. And by the grace of God, we stumble out!

The movie *Shadowlands* is a powerful story of the "little resurrections" that are possible while we wait for the big one yet to be. The movie is based on the short-lived marriage of C. S. Lewis and Joy Davidman. Lewis was a hardened intellectual until Davidman came into his life and taught him to love again. Then she died tragically at a young age of cancer.

In the final scene of the movie, Lewis is sitting with Davidman's young son, Douglas, now in his care. They are sitting before the wardrobe closet that provided a passageway into imaginary worlds in Lewis's novels for children. Devastated by the loss of his mother, Douglas says, "I thought prayer would save her. But it doesn't work."

"No, it doesn't work," says Lewis.

"I don't care," the boy says defiantly.

Lewis searches for words: "I loved your mother very much," he ventures. "Perhaps I loved her too much. . . . It doesn't seem fair does it?"

"I don't see why she had to get sick," says the boy.

"No, nor me. But you can't hold onto things, Douglas. You have to let them go."

"Jack," says the boy, using Lewis's nickname, "do you believe in heaven?"

There is a long pause as Lewis searches his heart: "Yes, I do."

In an angry, broken voice, the boy cries out, "I don't believe in heaven."

"That's okay," says Lewis.

"I sure would like to see her again," says Douglas.

His eyes brimming with tears, Lewis begins to sob, something he hasn't done since losing his own mother as a boy. "Me too," he wails, then he clutches the boy, and they cry in each other's arms.

That scene symbolizes the resurrection of C. S. Lewis, transformed from an unfeeling, hardened soul into a sensitive, loving man by the pain of losing someone he held dear. The movie closes with his reminiscence: "Why love if loving hurts so much? I have only the life I've lived. Two times I've had that choice. As a boy and as a man. The boy chose safety. The man chooses suffering. The pain now is part of the happiness then. That's the deal."

This side of God's eternity, that's the deal. Mary and Martha got their loved one back; we do not. What we get instead is Jesus' assurance that those who die trusting in him step from death's darkness into the fullness of God's light. While we cannot get them back, we can get our life back, enriched and deepened. And given the wrenching losses from which some have risen in the power of Christ's living presence, who's to say which is the greater miracle?

The poet John Donne confessed, "I have committed a grave sin. Where Lazarus spent four days, I have spent forty years." It need not be so. For Jesus Christ yet has the power to awaken us to life. Listen for his voice, and heed his call. No matter how deep your tomb of despair and desperation, he is calling for you.

Gracious God, thank you for the tears—
both yours and ours—that make the hurt bearable,
until in your nearer presence, we can at last let it go.
In Jesus' name we pray; so help us live
in the power of his risen presence.
Amen.

Questions for Reflection

1. Can you remember a time when you felt ignored and forgotten by Jesus? Are you at such a place now? How does the story of Lazarus, Mary, and Martha illuminate your own experience?
2. Do you agree that "love complicates the life of God"? How would the world be different if God were an indulgent parent catering to our every whim?
3. Jesus refers to death as "falling asleep" (11:11), a phrase that appears elsewhere in the New Testament (1 Corinthians 15:51; 1 Thessalonians 4:14; see KJV since the NRSV here paraphrases the Greek word for "sleep" as "death"). What makes sleep a fitting metaphor for those who have died in faith?

4. Consider how John 10—the Good Shepherd laying down his life for the sheep (v. 11)—and John 11—the raising of Lazarus—foreshadow the death and resurrection of Jesus. What does it suggest about God that not just Lazarus, but God's one and only Son, was interred in a tomb?
5. Some Christians believe that showing grief manifests a lack of faith. How does the story of Jesus at Lazarus' tomb challenge this notion?
6. In what ways is the Lazarus story a commentary on Jesus' power to give eternal life now (see John 3:15-16, 36; 4:14; 5:21-26; 6:47-58; 10:10; 11:25; 17:3)? Can you name some of the "little resurrections" in your own life that point to the larger resurrection yet to be?

CHAPTER 12

Unless a Seed Dies

John 12:20-33

In the late fourth century, a monk named Telemachus went to the desert to pray. While he was there, God stirred his heart about an evil thriving in faraway Rome. Though the empire was now officially Christian, gladiators still fought to the death in the Roman arena. So Telemachus left his desert hideaway and made his way to Rome.

There he found eighty thousand roaring fans eager to see gladiators fight and die. The little monk was appalled to see an allegedly Christian populace swollen with blood lust. He watched in horror as the gladiators raised their swords and shouted, "Hail, Caesar! We who are about to die salute you!" while frenzied crowds cheered them on.

Telemachus couldn't bear to see such butchery unleashed, so he leaped over the wall and ran into the arena. He put himself between two warriors, and for a moment they were startled into submission. But the crowd began to hiss and boo. "Be rid of him!" they cried. "Let the games begin!"

The gladiators pushed the old man aside, but he again came between them. The crowd then started hurling stones at the monk, who was still outfitted in his hermit's robe. They shouted for the gladiators to kill the one hindering their fun. At last the commander gave the nod. With the flash of a gladiator's sword, the holy man lay dead.

Suddenly the frenzied mob fell silent. They looked in horror at what their savage instincts had wrought. Stunned onlookers shook their heads in disbelief. One by one they turned to leave, until at last the great stadium was empty.

After that terrible day, no gladiator ever raised his sword to the amusement of a crowd, for the Roman games ended that day never to start again.[1]

"Unless a grain of wheat falls into the earth and dies, it remains just a single grain; but if it dies, it bears much fruit" (12:24). It is a principle etched in history: dying for a just cause can have a profound effect. As Gibbon said of the monk Telemachus, "His death was more useful . . . than his life."[2]

One thinks also of Socrates calmly drinking his hemlock. His courage in the face of death multiplied the power of his philosophy. Or what of Joan of Arc, whose tragic death lit a fire of French patriotism and piety? And then there was William Tyndale, burned at the stake in 1526 for translating the Bible into English. A short century later the King James Bible rose from the ashes of that debacle. Again and again, Jesus' words have proven true: "Unless a seed dies, it remains a single grain. But if it dies, it bears much fruit."

At last, that moment came for Jesus—the moment when he realized that to go on living would reduce him to a footnote in history. Yes, he might be remembered as a gifted itinerant teacher who shook things up a bit in first-century Palestine. He might warrant a mention in the encyclopedia as one of the world's great sages. But he would never become the world's *Savior* until he kept his rendezvous with a Roman cross and allowed the atoning love of God to flow.

Contemplating what provoked that realization is frightening, at least in John's Gospel. For it came in response to a request from some Greeks who were in town for the Jewish festival of Passover. In a sense, those Greek visitors were the emissaries for all Gentiles seeking an audience with Jesus.

---

[1] William Barclay, *The Gospel of Mark,* rev. ed. (Philadelphia: Westminster, 1975), 204-5.

[2] Ibid., 205.

Apparently they had done their homework, for they knew that with the rarest of exceptions, Jesus confined his ministry to his own people, the Jews.

Once, when a Gentile woman pressed him for help, Jesus had the gall to say, "It's not right to take the children's food and give it to the dogs."

Whereupon the woman shot back, "That may be, Lord, but even the dogs get to eat the crumbs under the table."

"True enough," said Jesus. Then he did as she asked (Mark 7:24-30).

Prior to this climactic moment in John's Gospel, that was about as close as Jesus got to helping Gentiles—which was not exactly enough to inspire confidence. Little wonder then that those Greek visitors, unsure of their ground, sought Philip's help. He was the natural choice, since his name was Greek and he hailed from Galilee where Greek influence was strong.

"Sir," they said to him, "we wish to see Jesus."

Philip, realizing this was a sensitive subject, sought out Andrew, whose name was Greek also. Together they screwed up their courage and went to Jesus.

"Lord, we know you like to keep to your own, but there's some really nice folks here from Athens who want to meet you. What shall we tell them?"

It was then that Jesus looked wistfully into heaven, nodded, and said, "The hour has come for the Son of Man to be glorified. Very truly, I tell you, unless a grain of wheat falls into the earth and dies, it remains just a single grain; but if it dies, it bears much fruit" (12:23-24).

Remember being in the fourth grade and falling for that love god or goddess three rows over? Not sure how to approach the object of your passion, you wrote a note with one of those big pencils, the size of a cigar. Then you tapped a neighbor on the shoulder and whispered, "How 'bout passing this over to Larry [or Sue or whomever]." You waited breathlessly as your note traveled across a succession of classmates like a rock skipping over a pond until at last it reached the boy or girl of your dreams. He or she opened the note and read, "Do you love me? Check yes or no." Long before the note came back, you knew from your beloved's smile or wince whether you had found a place in his or her heart.

In John 12 we see certain Greeks scribbling their love note to Jesus. They pass it to Philip, Philip passes it to Andrew, and Andrew passes it to Jesus. And when Jesus opens the note, we see him nodding. Suddenly our hearts skip a beat because we know he is going to check "yes." "Yes, I love you."

Only we don't yet understand the depths of this love, for in checking the "yes" box, Jesus has elected to die. That is what it would take for his love to reach past his own people and his own time all the way to us.

Yes, because some out-of-towners started knocking on the door of his kingdom, our Lord saw the fateful moment had come: "The hour has come for the Son of Man to be glorified" (12:23). Yet what a strange glory this is, for in the Fourth Gospel, Jesus' "glory" is a code word for his death.[3] Only as the Savior dies, like a seed appearing to perish in the ground, will the promise of his life come to full flower.

And just in case we're inclined to believe this was an easy decision for Jesus, John pulls back the curtains just a bit and lets us peek at our Lord's humanity. "Now my soul is troubled. And what should I say—'Father, save me from this hour'?" (12:27). Here we see even John's Jesus, usually bigger than life, struggling to be faithful to his calling. Yet, as always, our Lord's homing instinct for God held true: "No, it is for this reason that I have come to this hour. Father, glorify your name" (12:27-28).

Then a voice from heaven sounded. "I have glorified it, and I will glorify it again." Standing nearby, some mistook the noise for thunder, and others, the cry of an angel. But Jesus immediately directed the crowd's attention to God. "This voice has come for your sake, not for mine" (12:30)—which is to say, it was and is crucial to recognize the uniqueness of Jesus' union with God. Herein lies the secret to his glory on the cross. Because Jesus and the Father are one, Jesus' death is not merely telling us about *him*. His death is a window into the very heart of God.

---

3 In addition to 12:23, 27-28, see also John 13:31-32 and 17:1-5.

And here the death of Jesus parts company with the death of Socrates, Joan of Arc, or any other of history's fallen heroes. For the power of Jesus' death rests not merely in the inspirational story of a good man dying for a just cause. The power of the cross rests in the realization that it was not just Jesus who hung there, but the broken heart of God.

Thus, we see an answer taking shape to the seemingly benign request, "Sir, we wish to see Jesus." Those Greek visitors—as perhaps we ourselves—merely wanted to see Jesus as a historical curiosity. They wanted to see what he looked like, hear the timbre of his voice, and look into his eyes. If we are only interested in Jesus at that level, then we might as well dispense with the New Testament, for it is gloriously indifferent to such matters.

But if we want to "see Jesus" at a deeper level—at a level that opens our eyes to his glory on the cross—then we must dare to believe that in Jesus of Nazareth, God's own self has drawn near. As Paul thunders in 2 Corinthians 5:19, "God was in Christ, reconciling the world unto himself" (KJV).

Not long ago, a man told me of a harrowing experience. "My heart stopped on the table in 1983," he said. "I was a different person after that."

Dare we say that at the cross of Jesus Christ, God's heart "stopped" on the table? God's best and brightest Son was strung up to die by a broken world. But rather than strike out in atoning rage, the Almighty crumpled in atoning love. God's very heart quivered and shook, stunned by the force of human depravity and sin. But when by some miracle of grace God's broken heart started beating again, it was coursing with a chastened love that would never die.

"Unless a grain of wheat falls into the earth and dies, it remains just a single grain; but if it dies, it bears much fruit" (12:24).

Because Jesus was one with the heart of God, his death can never be reduced to the death of a martyr dying for a just and noble cause. It was that, but it was so much more. Nor can we accept the pernicious notion that a loving Jesus died to appease a vengeful God who demanded a blood bounty as the cost of divine forgiveness. *No!* It was our loving Creator, uniquely present in Jesus Christ, who suffered on that cross. And when God's only Son died there, it was God's great heart that trembled, shook, and then issued in an outpouring of atoning love.

Ian Pitt-Watson relates a story told by a seminarian. The student's name was Bill, and as a young boy, Bill became an avid fan of golf. Wanting to encourage his interest, his parents bought him some plastic balls and clubs. But since the driving range was the backyard, Bill was told that real golf balls were off limits.

Bill quickly got the knack of hitting the plastic balls and developed a good swing. But soon he was hankering to hear the click of a real golf ball against his club. Finally, he let temptation overwhelm him. He got a golf ball from his father's bag, teed up, and hit it with all his strength.

Unfortunately, the ball hooked sharply and headed for the house. There was a loud crash as the ball shattered a window. Even worse, the crash was followed by a piercing scream.

In a panic, Bill ran to the house and burst into the living room. There standing before the broken window was his mother with blood on her face. The boy looked in horror at the injury he had caused.

Finally, he was able to gasp, "Oh, Mother, *Mother*, what have I done?"

She turned to him and said, "Don't worry, son. I'm going to be all right."

At that, the distraught boy began to whimper, and the mother took him in her arms.

Reflecting on the experience years later, Bill said that seeing his mother bleeding because of his transgression affected him profoundly. Never again could he so callously disobey her directions. The sight of his mother standing before that broken window with blood on her face, all because of *him*, changed the boy forever.[4]

---

4 *Parables, etc.* 7, no. 2 (February 1987), 4.

In the end, it was as Jesus said: "I, when I am lifted up . . . , will draw all people to myself" (12:32). Seeing him bloodied because of us changes everything. To be sure, his life was beautiful and true. But it was his death that revealed the truth about us—namely, that apart from God's guidance and grace, we are capable of shameless evil.

It was supremely Jesus' death that revealed the truth about God: no matter how grievous or ghastly our sin, God loves us still. And though the costs of such love are staggering, our Lord won't let us go.

That is the glory of God revealed at the cross of Jesus Christ. It is not the glory of God's brilliance. It is not the glory of God's power. It is the glory of God's atoning love. It is the glory of a God who will stop at nothing to embrace and forgive wayward children. And once you have seen that glory shining from the face of the Crucified One, nothing can ever be the same again.

"Sir, we would see Jesus." The Greek visitors didn't know what they were asking, but because of their innocent request, Jesus turned toward his cross. And there he planted the seed of his life and love in every believing heart.

O holy Christ, we would see you also—
not as a historical curiosity, but as our crucified
and risen Lord. Call forth from our chastened,
broken hearts faith and true repentance.
Amen.

Questions for Reflection

1. What did Jesus mean by the strange statement, "Those who love their life lose it, and those who hate their life in this world will keep it for eternal life" (12:25)? Is Jesus encouraging his followers to feign or to cultivate low self-esteem?
2. Can you think of a time when you "died" to selfish ambition and your sacrifice redounded to good? How does that experience illustrate the power of self-surrender in Jesus'

teaching? Besides John 12:25, see also Matthew 16:25; Mark 8:35; Luke 9:24; and 17:33.

3. Many Christian pulpits are inscribed with the words, "Sir, we would see Jesus" (12:21, KJV). Ponder how the request made of Philip is a challenge to every believer. What allows others to see Jesus in us?

4. John 12:27-28 is sometimes called John's Gethsemane (cf. Matthew 26:36-46; Mark 14:32-42). Why was his version of Jesus' struggle so brief? Why was it pivotally important that he include it nonetheless?

5. The quality of a harvest is directly related to the quality of the seed that produces it. What was it about Jesus that made his death qualitatively different from that of other martyrs struck down by evil?

6. Did Jesus have to die to save the world? What if everyone had responded positively to his message? Or was that even possible given the broken world into which he came (3:19-20)?

7. What role, if any, did Jesus' cross play in drawing you to him? In your own spiritual autobiography, does Jesus' saying ring true: "I, when I am lifted up from the earth, will draw all people to myself" (12:32). If not, what drew you—or draws you—to Jesus?

Trailmarker

A fter the raising of Lazarus, the undisputed power of Jesus' words and deeds made him a force to be reckoned with. His enemies decided he had to be eliminated lest he rob them entirely of religious and political clout (11:45-53). As Jesus saw the shadow of his cross drawing near, he faced the prospect of an unjust death with resolute courage (12:23-32).

Before Jesus was wrested away from his disciples, he took pains to prepare them for the gathering storm. This is seen first at the Last Supper where, in washing his disciples' feet, he anticipated the lavish outpouring of love from his cross (chap. 13). Then after Judas left to betray him, Jesus set about preparing his disciples for the reality of his death and the gift of his continuing presence in the wake of his Easter rising (chaps. 14–16). This section of the Gospel closes with Jesus' moving prayer for himself (17:1-5), his disciples (17:6-19), and for all who would someday come to know and love him (17:20-26).

When this intimate discourse was complete, the meditative mood was shattered by the approach of storm troopers and the rattle of torches and swords (18:3). And for a while, Jesus' disciples forgot everything he had told them.

But after Easter—when the promise of John 14–16 proved true—John reconstructed the words and wrote them down so that forever after believers would know where to find peace at the eye of the storm (16:33).

CHAPTER 13

God's Heartbeat in Our Souls

John 14:1-27

"Do not let your hearts be troubled"! That seems a stretch for a bunch of guys shattered by the realization their Lord is about to die.

In John 13, Jesus has thrown in the towel, literally and figuratively. He has washed his disciples' feet and tried to prepare them for the grim events that lie ahead.

Now as chapter 14 opens, Jesus' disciples are still reeling from the news that their Master is leaving them in the lurch. All the dreams, spoken and unspoken, they have pinned on him, are gone. All their hopes have been vaporized. And now he has the gall to tell them, "Do not let your hearts be troubled"? It sounds depressingly similar to the misguided counsel many bereaved persons must endure: "Keep your chin up." "It's for the best." "Time heals all wounds."

One can feel the shock and tension on the rise as Jesus plows ahead: "In my Father's house there are many dwelling places. If it were not so, would I have told you that I go to prepare a place for you?"

But the disciples just stare at him forlornly, because all that talk about the "Sweet Bye and Bye" just doesn't touch them where they are living *now*. They want to know how they're going to make it through the day after tomorrow, not how they're going to live in heavenly bliss at some vague point in the future. Slowly, like milk nearing the boiling point, their bewilderment is curdling toward anger.

So when Jesus makes the lofty, even presumptuous comment, "You know the way to the place where I am going," Thomas nails him on it. "Lord," he says, in an angry, accusing tone, "we don't have a clue where you are going. So how can we possibly know the way?"

Jesus matches Thomas's glare, eyeball for eyeball, then peers past his pupils into his heart. "You know the way, Thomas," Jesus reassures him, "because you know *me. I* am the way, the truth, and the life."

And suddenly we discover: Christianity isn't about having the answers. It's about being held by a love so large that unanswered questions hold neither terror nor shame.

But like Thomas, most people are looking for abstract answers they can then relate to Jesus. What is the nature of Ultimate Reality, and how does Jesus fit in? What does it mean to be fully human, and how does Jesus reveal—or fall short of—this theoretical ideal? What do near-death experiences suggest about the character and dimensions of the "Father's house"? In Thomas's words, "Show us *where you are going*—the destination of the spiritual pilgrimage—and then we'll know how to make sense of you." Or as Philip puts it in his follow-up, "Show us the Father, and we will be satisfied" (14:8).

In other words, let's start with *GOD*, Jesus, and in due time, we'll get to you.

The pain of rejection showing in his eyes, Jesus answers, "Don't you get it by now, Philip? If you have seen me, you have seen the Father." Then wistfully, he adds, "So how can you sit there and say to me, 'Show us the Father.'" (14:9)

Even after months and years of the most intimate communion, Jesus' disciples don't "get it." They don't understand that following him is not some kind of extracurricular activity to be tacked on to the life of faith; it is the core curriculum, the heart of the learning, the door opening into the larger mystery of God.[1]

---

[1] Cf. John 10:9, KJV.

The great missionary–evangelist E. Stanley Jones told of a missionary lost in an African jungle. After wandering in the bush for hours on end, he finally happened upon a native hut. To the missionary's great relief, the tribesman agreed to lead him to civilization.

For more than an hour, the native cut and hacked his way through the dense undergrowth. Finally, worried that perhaps his guide was unreliable, the missionary said to him, "Are you quite sure this is the way? I see no path."

"Bwana," the native answered. "In this place there is no path. *I* am the path. Follow me!"[2]

Christianity does not begin with a spiritual road map that exists in abstract speculation. Christianity begins with the Master's concrete command, "Follow me," for at its heart, Christianity is "a way" embodied in a person—the person of Jesus Christ. In due time that "way" becomes a "truth," and the truth becomes a "life." But it begins with the willingness to follow the One in whose face shines the very glory of God (2 Corinthians 4:6).

We cannot begin with figuring out who God is and then somehow relate that to Jesus, because we don't know who God is until we see God's life and love and likeness revealed in Jesus called Christ. Thus, Christianity begins with the conviction, or at least the hope, that God's decisive self-disclosure was made in a first-century Jewish carpenter from Nazareth.

Realizing his disciples were scandalized by his audacious pronouncements—as many still are today—Jesus began unpacking the meaning of the statement, "Whoever has seen me has seen the Father." And he did so by exploring the mutual indwelling that existed between the Father and the Son: "I am in the Father and the Father is in me" (14:10).

The essence of Jesus' words and works are uniquely, decisively revealing, because the most intimate union exists between himself and the eternal God: it is a union of purpose, will, and, yes, even being.

Granted, that is a shocking and revolutionary claim. It is far more than the Bible claims for Abraham, Sarah, Moses,

---

2 *The Pastor's Story File,* April 1985, Volume 1, No. 4, p 1.

Miriam, David, Esther, or any other spiritual giant within its pages. But it is the intent of John's Gospel to claim nothing less, for this Gospel is forged on the conviction that while "no one has ever seen God, . . . God the only Son, who is close to the Father's heart, . . . has made him known" (1:18).

Given the intimate union that exists between Jesus and God, to "see" Jesus—not just as an interesting historical figure, but as the Lord of life—is to see God. For Jesus is the face of the Eternal poking into time, the light of God spilling into history. By looking to him, we see into the larger mystery of the Divine.

This is not to say God can be reduced to Jesus, or said differently, that Jesus is "all" of God.[3] God is "bigger" than Jesus, even as one's face is but the entry point into the larger mystery of his or her person. But whatever mysteries lie beyond the face of God revealed in Jesus Christ, they do not contradict the essential character of God as we have seen it disclosed in Jesus. To the crucial question, "What is God like?" the Christian knows but one answer: "God is like Jesus."

Thus, Jesus calms his disciples by telling them first of all that they have nothing to fear. Even if death temporarily snatches him from them, they can face the void of his absence in the assurance that God is faithful love, for that is the God they have seen embodied and revealed in him. Even if the "light of the world" is temporarily extinguished and night falls upon the earth, his witness remains the North Star of the Spirit. What he has said and who he is remains the only fixed star in an ever-changing sky; always, he points unerringly toward God.

Yet there is more. For even if Jesus must go away, they will not be left "orphaned" (14:18). He himself will come to them in the presence of the "Advocate," the very life and love of God indwelling the believing heart.

> "I will ask the Father, and he will give you another Advocate, to be with you forever. This is the Spirit of truth, whom the world cannot receive, because it neither sees

---

3 Cf. 14:28: "The Father is greater than I."

him nor knows him. You know him, because he abides
with you, and he will be in you" (14:16–18).

Here Jesus speaks of the Holy Spirit, whom he calls the "Advocate," or the "Comforter," or the "Counselor," depending on
one's translation. These are all attempts to translate the same
Greek word—*Paraclete*—which means literally, "One called in
to help." It refers to someone summoned to the side of another
to befriend, encourage, and if necessary, plead that person's
cause. The Holy Spirit reveals himself in a multitude of ways,
depending on the help that is needed.

Dietrich Bonhoeffer was a German pastor and theologian
who died in a Nazi concentration camp because he confessed
Christ, and not the Führer, as Lord. He wrote in one of his journals of a night when his own strength was sapped and the Holy
Spirit came to see him through.

> I vividly recall that night of torture, and how I prayed
> to God that he might send death to deliver me because
> of the hopelessness and pain I felt I could no longer
> endure. How I wrestled with God that night and finally,
> in my great need, crept to him weeping. Not until
> morning did a great peace come to me, a blissful aware-
> ness of light, strength, and warmth, bringing with it the
> conviction that I must see this thing through. Solace in
> woe. This is the Holy Spirit, the Comforter, which
> enables a man to live and endure.[4]

Most believers can remember such a time when they were
steadied and steeled by an unseen Presence. Ready to give up,
they felt the strength to go on crystallize within them, a sheer
gift of grace. Unsure of where to turn or what to do, a shaft of
illumination pierced their darkness, and they saw the next step.
Pulled kicking and screaming into a future they didn't want to
face, they stumbled into the eye of the storm and, incredibly, at
the center of the terror, found calmness, confidence, and peace.

---

[4] Dietrich Bonhoeffer, quoted in *Pulpit Resource*, Vol. 7, No. 2, April-June, 1979, p. 30.

Such are the signs of the Spirit's presence. Our Lord does not leave us "orphaned" (NRSV) or "comfortless" (KJV); rather, clothed in the wings of the Spirit, he ever draws near to help—not as some vague, impersonal force, like electricity recharging a battery, but as the very life of God indwelling and renewing us.

There is a strange, unsettling beauty about all the promises running together in John 14. First, Jesus assures us that to know him is to know the Father (v. 9). Then he tells us he will be mysteriously present in the work of the Holy Spirit (vv. 17-18). Finally, he says that both the Father *and* the Son will indwell the believer through the Spirit: "Those who love me will keep my word, and my Father will love them, and *we* will come to them and make *our* home with them" (v. 23, my emphasis).

Like it or not, we are wading here into the deep waters of the Trinity, the Church's confession that God is a threefold union of Father, Son, and Holy Spirit. Granted, while the New Testament does not contain a full-blown trinitarian doctrine, it is filled with trinitarian language.[5] In fact, just try to make sense of the rich tapestry of truths in John chapters 14–16 without some such notion of God's three-in-oneness. It is impossible without denying the full divinity of either the Son or the Spirit—or the oneness of God—which the Church refused to do. Instead, the Church settled for the essential if unwieldy confession that the God who encounters us in Jesus Christ is not a flat, one-dimensional God, but a lively communion of love: Father, Son, and Holy Spirit.

Thus, to know the Son is to know the Father is to know the Spirit. The three can be separated for purposes of discussion, much as a jeweler might look at each facet of a diamond in turn. But it is the *same* diamond, brilliant with light. Even so, through faith in Christ, the believer is ushered into a living union with God the Father in the power of God the Holy Spirit.

The Church father Tertullian conceived a brilliant analogy for expressing the Christian experience of God. Imagine God the Father as the sun, the source of all light and life. God the

---

5 Matthew 28:19–20, 2 Corinthians 13:13, and Ephesians 4:4–6 are but a few of the many passages that could be cited.

Son is akin to the sunbeam going forth from God, bringing light and truth. God the Holy Spirit is the warmth of the sunbeam striking one's face. And yet the sunbeam touching the face is intimately bound to the sun from which it sprang.

Even so, God the Father sends forth God the Son to communicate his personal warmth and presence in God the Holy Spirit. But God's "threeness" is ever bound together by a larger Oneness.

Do such mind-boggling ideas and analogies really matter? Yes, to the extent that they drive home the conviction weaving its way through John 14 that while Jesus, a person lodged within history, may be leaving his disciples, he will be with them in Spirit forevermore. "Spirit" here is not used as we use the word today to mean the lingering influence of someone who is deceased: "While Aunt Ida may be gone, we'll feel her 'spirit' always." Rather, it means the life-giving, indwelling, personal presence of God in every believing heart. It is this blessed gift that Jesus died to bestow in the wake of his Easter rising. For finally, it was through his life, death, and resurrection that the ancient promise proved true:

> The days are surely coming, says the LORD, when I will make a new covenant with the house of Israel and the house of Judah . . . I will put my law within them, and I will write it on their hearts; and I will be their God, and they shall be my people. No longer shall they teach one another, or say to each other, "Know the LORD," for they shall all know me, from the least of them to the greatest, says the LORD; for I will forgive their iniquity, and remember their sin no more. (Jeremiah 31:31–34)

In a large metropolitan hospital, there was a constant problem with noise in the nursery. At times the crying level among the newborns reached heights that were unbearable for both the staff and the babies. The administration tried separating the infants and soundproofing the walls. While this brought relief to the nurses, it didn't seem to calm the infants.

Finally, someone hit upon the idea of playing a recording of a mother's heartbeat inside each crib. It worked! At last the newborns were at peace, calmed by a sound that recalled the security of their mother's womb.

The Holy Spirit is God's heartbeat in our souls—the ground of our assurance that nothing in heaven or on earth can separate us from the love of God in Jesus Christ our Lord. The Spirit is the wellspring of that peace Jesus said he would give, that the world can never take away (14:27).

Thus, the discourse in John 14 draws to a close[6] much as it begins: "Do not let your hearts be troubled, and do not let them be afraid" (v. 27). Only now we know that Jesus was not engaging in cliché-popping consolation. He was simply stating the awesome new reality his death and resurrection would make possible: an uncanny calm in the eye of every storm. No longer would his disciples follow him in their own strength, but in the strength of Another: the Holy Spirit, the Comforter, the Advocate—the very life and love of God beating in their souls.

Come, Holy Spirit, breath of the living God:
renew and invigorate us, we pray.
Give us the longing and the will to follow Jesus
that in following him we might be drawn ever deeper
into fellowship with the One he called "Father."
In his name we ask it to the glory of the Father,
the Son, and the Holy Spirit, one God, now and forever.
Amen.

Questions for Reflection

1. Thomas contested Jesus' statement, "You know the way to the place where I am going" (14:4). Was Jesus wrong, or did Thomas and the others "know" more than they realized?

---

6 While chapter 14 ends with the words, "Rise, let us be on our way," the themes of this chapter are more fully explored in chapters 15 and 16. These three chapters are best read as one continuous narrative.

2. Do you agree that Christianity is first a "way," then a "truth" and a "life" (14:6)? Or do some people come to Christ first through his "truth" or his "life"? How would you track your own Christian experience using these categories?

3. Does Jesus' statement, "No one comes to the Father except through me" (14:6) mean that to know God, a conscious affirmation of Jesus as Lord is required? Or simply that all true knowledge of God must be consistent with what we see revealed of God in Jesus? What biblical evidence can you muster to support your answer?

4. Do you agree that John 14 (along with chapters 15–16) cries out for some notion of the Trinity? If so, then why is the Trinity seen as awkward, even expendable, by many modern Christians? If not, how do you make sense of the unique union of God, Jesus, and the Holy Spirit claimed in these verses?

5. Some groups—Jehovah's Witnesses and Mormons among them—claim the Holy Spirit is a divine *power*, but not the divine *presence*. How do John chapters 14–16 present the Holy Spirit as a fully personal presence of the Divine? See especially John 14:15–17; 14:26; 15:26–27; 16:7–11; 16:12–14, and note the use of personal pronouns. What rides on this distinction between "presence" and "power"?

CHAPTER 14

Being Jesus or Being *in* Jesus?

John 15:1-11

James ("Quick") Tillis was an Oklahoma cowboy who began his boxing career in Chicago. He recalls being quickly cut down to size upon his arrival in the Windy City.

"I got off the bus from Tulsa with two cardboard suitcases under my arms in downtown Chicago, and stopped in front of the Sears Tower. I put my suitcases down and I looked up at the tower and said to myself, 'I'm going to conquer Chicago.'"

"When I looked back down, the suitcases were gone."[1]

Armed with high hopes and burning resolve, perhaps we also expected great things to happen: a rebellious adolescent brought under control, an intractable problem solved, a life-long compulsion finally conquered. And yet after tackling the challenge at hand with everything within us, we had little or nothing to show for our efforts. Perhaps like Mr. Tillis, a bloated sense of self-importance blinded us to the sizeable difficulties we faced. But sooner or later most of us receive some sort of wake-up call that we are not so all-sufficient as we like to imagine.

Jesus knew his disciples would be sorely tempted to pursue the work of his kingdom in their own strength. Yet he also knew that if they did, their efforts would come to naught. So shortly before leaving to face his cross, he warned them in

---

[1] *Parables, etc.* Volume 13, No. 5, p. 3 (May 1993).

the strongest possible terms: "Apart from me you can do nothing" (15:5). He didn't say, "Without me you can do *very little*, or *less than your best*, or *nothing of any consequence.*" No, seeing the challenges that lay ahead, the Master went for broke: "Apart from me you can do *nothing!*"

Then, to press the point home, Jesus drew on the image of a vine and its branches. It was a familiar figure to his disciples, for in the Old Testament, Israel was often likened to a vine.[2] Here Jesus proclaims himself the "true vine," the one in whom God's presence is decisively revealed (15:1). His disciples are but branches springing from the taproot of his own life with God, while the Father is the overseer, or "vinegrower," of the whole operation.

"Abiding"[3] is the word Jesus uses to describe the believer's vital relationship to him; it is a word that appears ten times in verses 4-10 alone; in John 14 the same word is used to describe the intimate union that exists between the Father and the Son.[4] Now the circle of their love is widened to include the believer also: "Abide in me as I abide in you" (15:4).

To abide in Christ is to be in vital communion with him through the power of the Holy Spirit. The life-giving flow of Christ's presence sustains and strengthens the disciple, much as a vine supports its branches: "Those who abide in me and I in them bear much fruit" (15:5). By contrast, when that relationship is cut off or compromised, the disciple becomes a withered branch starving for sustenance and life (15:6).

Somewhere I read about a little water spider that lives beneath the surface of a pond in a kind of diver's bell. He makes a thimble-shaped house of silk, which he anchors by fine threads to the pond's bottom. The opening of this tiny dwelling faces downward. The spider then goes to the surface, and by means of hooked hairs that cover the lower part of his body, entraps a bubble of air, which he carries down and

---

2 See, e.g., Psalm 80:8-16; Isaiah 5:1-7; Jeremiah 2:21; Ezekiel 19:10-14.

3 The Greek word *meno* is variously translated as "abide," "remain," "indwell," "reside."

4 In John 14 variations of the Greek root word *meno* appear in vv. 10, 16, 17, and 25.

releases inside his subterranean abode. He repeats this journey until all the water in his silk thimble house is gradually displaced by the air he brings. Then he goes about his work in the house, and when he has exhausted all his oxygen, he goes up for more. So it is that he maintains his life in an alien environment only by ceaseless vigilance.

In like manner, the Christian is called to attend to the vertical dimension of his or her life. Only through communion with the living Christ can he or she get the spiritual oxygen required to live as Christ's disciple in a sometimes hostile world.[5] Only as we cling to Christ in faith and devotion, abiding in him as a branch draws its life from the vine, can he call forth the fruit of his Spirit in and through us. Thus, Jesus' solemn warning—"Apart from me you can do nothing"—was meant not as a threat, but as a gracious invitation to commune with him who is the source of our life.

The question then becomes, "*How* does one abide in Christ?" How do we maintain that living union with him that allows us to flourish and grow as his disciples? One answer Jesus suggests is that centering ourselves upon him requires a certain pruning: "Every branch that bears fruit [the Father] prunes to make it bear more fruit (15:2)." When a plant is pruned, the branches or limbs remaining are driven back to their source, thereby becoming vital and strong. An unpruned plant grows wildly in all directions until its strength is sapped and its form destroyed.

So often, my life resembles a plant in need of pruning. How quickly the demands and pressures seem to multiply in all directions. Before I know it, I find myself overextended and rushing to keep up. And from talking with others, I know I am not alone in this dilemma. Retirees report they are busier than ever, and many younger people exhaust themselves pursuing career success while trying to be a supermom or superdad on the side. With a full appointment book and looming "to do" list staring us in the face, there seems precious little time to center on Christ and his will for our lives.

---

5 A theme more fully explored in 15:18-25.

Yet maintaining this maddening pace rarely yields the results we seek. It seems we work harder and harder for less and less, not only financially, but in every sphere of life. Others don't appreciate our efforts, the desire to help is met with resistance and even suspicion, and ambitious schemes for self-reform bear little fruit. We find ourselves empty, spent, and exhausted, a brittle branch, fragile and at the breaking point, devoid of vitality and life. Sometimes, in the pain of that realization, the Master's caution sounds: "Apart from me you can do nothing." And we are forced to concede that once again he is right.

How different life might be if communing with the living Christ were the first order of business and not the last. In her book *Beyond Chaos: Stress Relief for the Working Woman*, Sheila West suggests just such a strategy. Arguing that chronic stress is a response to the chaos and fragmentation of modern life, West proposes we clarify our life's purpose in the light of Christ's claim upon us. Doing so creates a sense of direction, order, and peace.

> One day while I was trying to visualize how purpose gives us meaning and direction in life, it occurred to me that purpose is also what gives us the freedom to be unique. I began connecting that to the function of DNA, [our] genetic coding material . . . It creates the building blocks that ensure all human beings have the same basic characteristics but also that each human being will be a unique individual.[6]

West goes on to develop that insight, suggesting that everyone's personhood and calling is unique, deriving from his or her spiritual "DNA." As she redefines the acronym, D stands for one's *direction,* God's purpose and will as revealed in Jesus Christ. N stands for one's *nature,* one's own unique personhood. And A stands for one's *actions,* those things we do— consistent with who we are—that move us toward fulfilling

---

6 Sheila West, *Beyond Chaos: Stress Relief for the Working Woman.* (NavPress, 1991). Quoted in a review in *Royal Service,* September 1993, 16-17.

God's purpose for our lives. By heeding our DNA—our direction, nature, and actions—we can enjoy both accomplishment and peace.

Perhaps every Christian who longs to "abide in Christ" and bear fruit in his name needs a "DNA" session each day. We need a time for consciously choosing among the many demands of our lives in the light of Christ's claim upon us. We need a pruning session, as it were, in which all that keeps Christ from blossoming and flowering within us can be cut away. Whether this quiet time of ordering our lives be the first thing we do in the morning or the last thing we do at night, is a matter of personal preference. But unless we systematically prune our lives of all that draws us away from our life with Christ, we will quickly become a barren branch, devoid of fruitfulness and life.

It appears from John 15 that such spiritual pruning is heavily dependent on "the word" of Jesus. Yes, sometimes the vine-grower prunes the branches directly, as when God uses the difficult circumstances of life to drive us back to Christ[7] (15:2). But one can also be "pruned" or "cleansed" by meditating directly upon Jesus' word (15:3). Indeed, it is in cherishing Jesus' word—probing its meaning and seeking its life-giving sustenance—that one demonstrates he or she is Jesus' disciple: "If you continue in my word, you are truly my disciples; and you will know the truth, and the truth will make you free" (8:31-32).

Jesus' "word" is both the whole of his teaching and the whole of his person; in him, as in no other, the medium and the message are one. Thus, for Christians today, letting Jesus' word "abide" in them means—at the very least—to be steeped in holy Scripture. For the Bible provides the authoritative witness to the saving deeds of God in the life of Israel (the Old Testament) and in the life, death, and resurrection of Jesus Christ (the New Testament).

---

[7] God does not send tragedy and loss but often moves within difficult circumstances. See, e.g., Romans 8:28 and Philippians 4:11-13.

Tragically, for many modern Christians, the regular reading of the Bible is not a staple of their spiritual diet. Yet apart from some such discipline, Christ remains a figment of our imagination instead of a living figure who speaks for himself. Apart from his word—which confronts us in the Bible, and supremely in the Gospels[8]—we are free to make of him whatever we will. Like a veteran returning with a war bride in tow, the relationship may appear to flourish so long as there is no real communication. While a language barrier exists, both husband and wife can imagine the other person to be whoever he or she wishes. Only as they learn to converse in a common language can each know the other as a real person rather than as a projection of one's own fantasies and needs.

Regular reading of the Bible allows Christ to emerge from the thicket of half-truths and fanciful assumptions, where we are inclined to keep him. And as he, the living Word, speaks through the written word of Scripture, we find that the confession of Hebrews 4:12 is true, sometimes painfully so: "The word of God is living and active, sharper than any two-edged sword, . . . able to judge the thoughts and intentions of the heart."

It is not unusual for the Bible to speak with uncanny relevance and power to the seeking heart. Christians believe that is because when the Bible is read in faith, the living Christ confronts us within its pages. Sometimes a particular passage speaks so clearly to our need, we can almost feel his breath as he whispers the words.

And then, beyond the pruning of our lives in response to his word, Jesus points us to the importance of prayer in maintaining a vital union with him: "If you abide in me, and my words abide in you, ask for whatever you wish, and it will be done for you" (15:7). Jesus was not about to entrust the power of prayer to those who would misuse it for selfish ends. So he prefaced his promise—"Ask for whatever you wish, and it will be done for you"—with the condition—"*If* you abide in me, and my words abide in you."

---

[8] The first four books of the New Testament: Matthew, Mark, Luke, and John.

To abide in Christ is to center ourselves upon him and his word. Having done that, we can no longer reduce prayer to a litany of favors sought or a sanctified wish list. Instead, it becomes our seeking of Christ's empowerment for the work he has for us to do.

One early contemplative, Saint Teresa of Avila, likened prayer to rain watering a garden.[9] No matter how well a garden is tended, unless God sends the rain to call forth the garden's bounty, it will remain dry and barren. Even so, having centered ourselves upon Christ and his word, we must yet seek the Spirit's enabling presence: "My Father is glorified by this, that you *bear much fruit* and become my disciples" (15:8).

And finally, having centered ourselves upon Christ's word, and having sought his presence and empowerment, we are ready to render loving service to others: "If you keep my commandments, you will abide in my love, just as I have kept my Father's commandments and abide in his love" (15:10). And "this is my commandment, that you love one another as I have loved you" (15:12). "Abiding in Christ" must never be reduced to losing oneself in mystical contemplation. Always, an authentic encounter with the living Christ makes one a channel of his love for others.

In one of his columns, the late Lewis Grizzard reminisced about his boyhood church. He remembered the youth group that met on Sunday nights and the two roughnecks required to attend by court order. They had broken into a local store and, as punishment, were forced to attend the youth group for the next six months.

The first night this unsavory twosome made their appearance, they beat up two other boys. And then when the session got started, they threw a hymnal at the nice lady leading the singing. Grizzard was particularly fond of this dear woman because she always brought the cookies. Fortunately, she managed to duck the flying hymnal just in time.

But years later Grizzard still remembered what she said to those boys. "I don't approve of what you boys did here tonight,

---

[9] As cited by Ben Campbell Johnson in *To Pray God's Will* (Philadelphia: Westminster Press, 1987), 28.

and neither does Jesus. But if he can forgive you, I guess I can too." Then she offered her home-baked cookies to the very scoundrels who had tried to deck her. The last Grizzard heard, those boys grew up to be "good daddies with steady jobs," who rarely missed a Sunday in that old frame church in Moreland, Georgia. Said Grizzard, "It was the first miracle I ever saw."[10]

That is the ultimate end of "abiding in Christ": to touch others with his love. After all, a vine and its branches don't exist merely to enjoy their union. They are bound together for a higher purpose, namely, to bear fruit.[11] Even so, a life lived in union with Jesus Christ cannot be contained. It inevitably reaches out to embrace a hurting, broken world.

Thankfully, following Jesus is not something we must do by the sheer dint of the will, but only as his abiding presence empowers us. As we endeavor to "abide in him," we receive the vision, courage, and strength we need for the journey of discipleship. Thankfully, we are not called to *be* Jesus, but to be *in* Jesus. After all, God has already provided the world a Savior. That means we can leave that mantle to another.

Our task is but to "grow in the grace and knowledge of our Lord and Savior Jesus Christ" (2 Peter 3:18). As we do, his life will take root and flower in our own. And out of the wonder of that union, we will be free to love others as we have been loved of God.

Thank you, O holy Christ,
for the power of your indwelling Spirit.
As we strive to abide in you, call forth the life
and love of God in us.
Make us instruments of your peace
to a broken world. To the glory
of the eternal One we pray.
Amen.

---

[10] As cited by Maxxie Dunnam, *This Is Christianity* (Nashville: Abingdon, 1994), 83-84.

[11] An emphasis found in verses 2, 4, 5, 8, and 16.

Questions for Reflection

1. What lessons can you draw from your own knowledge of gardening that might apply to "pruning" a life?
2. What does it mean to "bear fruit" according to the teaching in John 15? How does that meaning relate to the "fruit of the Spirit" listed in Galatians 5:22-23?
3. In 15:16, Jesus qualifies his emphasis on fruit-bearing to say "fruit that *will last.*" Why was this clarification necessary? And what might it suggest about the Church's ministry today?
4. Judas Iscariot is a tragic example of a branch that withered and was "thrown away" (15:6). Can you think of others? Who throws such branches "into the fire"?
5. What resources, if any, have been helpful to you in reading the Bible and learning to pray?
6. This chapter emphasizes personal devotion in the struggle to "abide in Christ." What role does corporate worship play in that quest? What else helps you "abide in Christ"?
7. Which more fully describes your understanding of Christian life: "following Jesus" or "abiding in Christ"?

Trailmarker

John 18:1–21:25

Following Jesus' discourse with his disciples (chaps. 14-16) and his moving prayer (chap. 17), John's Gospel shifts from meditation to action. After Judas leads a band of sanctified thugs to arrest Jesus (18:1-11), the plot quickly gathers momentum. Jesus is hauled first before the religious authorities where he faces a kangaroo court; he then faces charges before Pilate, the Roman governor of Judea. Unlike the religious establishment, Pilate appears to want to do the right thing; he just can't summon the courage. But throughout both trials—the religious and the civil—Jesus conducts himself with regal bearing. It appears Jesus' accusers, rather than he, are on trial.

But Jesus' trial is not about justice; it is about a deadly assault against the Son of God by the powers of darkness. Consequently, Jesus is condemned to die (chap. 19); yet from his cross his heavenly glory blazes brighter still. The One who descended to earth from the dizzying depths of the Godhead (1:1, 14) now descends into the dizzying depths of human depravity, darkness, and shame. Even there he is the "light shining in the darkness," for in his suffering and death he reveals a wounded, brokenhearted God that takes the worst a cruel, vicious world can devise, but loves it still.

Of course, no one this side of eternity would have known that apart from Jesus' resurrection. So John's Gospel concludes with the risen Lord returning to his disciples. Though robed once more in heavenly glory, he still bears the wounds of his costly engagement with a broken world (John 20). He graces his disciples with his forgiveness and peace. Then he bestows upon them the promised gift of the Holy Spirit (14:18-21, 25-27; 20:21-22), and the very life and love of God takes hold within them. Now at last they have "power" to become "sons and daughters of God" (1:12).

Curiously, John's Gospel appears to end at 20:30-31: "Now Jesus did many other signs in the presence of his disciples, which are not written in this book. But these are written so that you may come to believe that Jesus is the Messiah, the Son of God, and that through believing you may have life in his name." Despite this clear and fitting close to the book, one turns the page to find yet another chapter. What gives?

It seems that chapter 21 was added by a later hand: "This is the disciple who is testifying to these things and has written them, and *we* know that his testimony is true" (21:24). Probably, disciples of the author here included a bit of oral tradition that he—for whatever reason—left out of the first edition of his Gospel.[12] Or perhaps the "beloved disciple" penned this material himself.

In either event, whether it was his afterthought or another's, we can be grateful this chapter was added, for it contains one of the most moving and evocative resurrection stories in the Gospels.

---

[12] See n. 4 in the Introduction regarding the "Johannine school."

CHAPTER 15

What Is Truth?

John 18:28-19:16

Pilate worries me. He worries me because, of all the characters in the drama of Jesus' trial and death, he is most like me: a well-meaning, middle-class kind of guy just trying to do his job. Yet he signed the death warrant for the Savior of the world.

Pilate was the Roman governor of Judea from 26-37 C.E. He was an upper-level bureaucrat in a low-level post. As governor, he was a big shot. But Judea was hardly a plum in the Roman civil service. It was filled with religious fanatics who despised the Roman occupation. Then as now the region was a tinderbox of passions. A single spark could make the whole thing burst into flame.

Judea was the kind of place the Romans sent young bucks on the rise or weary old men who had outlived their usefulness. It was a rung on the corporate ladder, held briefly on one's way up or down. Pilate shows all the signs of a man in decline. His pitiful vacillation during the trial of Jesus suggests he was just biding his time till retirement. He was just trying to hold on until he could be delivered from the hell that was Palestine.

One morning, bright and early (18:28), a servant banged on the door. "Wake up, boss!" he shouted. "The natives are restless!"

Pilate groaned as he rolled over in bed. His head was pounding from a hangover. "Send them away!" he moaned. "Make an appointment for later."

"No can do, boss," the servant answered. "This is Passover, their biggest festival, and everything's in a stir. Now there's a mob at the door. I think you'd better handle this one yourself."

"All right!" Pilate snapped, throwing back the covers. "I'll be down as soon as I can." Thus, he was drawn into the most momentous event of his life, and he didn't even know it.

When Pilate finally faced the mob milling at his door, he discovered they were incensed with one Jesus of Nazareth. The ringleaders claimed this Jesus was trying to foment a rebellion against Rome. Usually such revolutionaries were national heroes. Why then had the accused fallen into such disfavor?

Not really interested, Pilate tried to pass the buck, encouraging the religious authorities to handle the matter themselves. But they wanted blood, and only the governor could decree death, so Pilate's hand was forced (18:31-32). Withdrawing into the palace, he asked the Galilean, "Are you a king like they say?"

"Who told you that?" Jesus answered.

"Who do ya think," Pilate spit out, his tone filling with acid. "I'm not a *Jew*. I don't care about your petty little quarrels. But your own leaders have turned you over to me, so fess up, boy. What have you done?"

Jesus answered, "My kingdom is not from this world. If it were, my followers would have fought to prevent my arrest."

"So you *are* a king?" Pilate pressed, his interest on the rise.

"Of a sort," Jesus answered, "but not the kind you think. I came to bear witness to the truth. Everyone who knows the truth listens to me."

It was then that Pilate stared at him blankly, threw up his hands, and said, "What is truth?" (18:38).

Imagine staring the very Son of God in the face and asking such a question. Here the light of God is streaming into Pilate's eyes, but he is so blind that the light falls helplessly against the door of his darkened heart. The King of the cosmos stands before him, but Pilate sees only a humble peasant he takes for a nobody. God's truth is sounding a wake-up call, but buried deep beneath the hardened cement of his own cynicism, Pilate doesn't hear a thing.

It's frightening to contemplate. What could possibly render one so oblivious to God's truth in Jesus? For if it was true of Pilate, it might also be true of us. Indeed, in some sense Pilate stands for all those who stare at Jesus not in anger, but in utter apathy. And such people are all about us. In our offices, in our civic clubs, in our families, maybe even in our churches. Perhaps we are such people ourselves. We're not *upset* with Jesus like those eager to string him up or tear him down. Rather, like Pilate, we greet him with a yawn.

Why did Jesus' truth arouse in Pilate neither hostility nor hope? Perhaps because Pilate lacked a spiritual center; he had no heart awake to the wonder and glory of God. The ultimate questions of life didn't interest him, nor did probing theological discussion. So when Jesus tried to reach Pilate, it was like a mountain climber throwing a rappelling hook into empty space. There was no place in Pilate's rock hard heart to which Jesus' words could grab and take hold.[1]

Thus, when Jesus told Pilate his kingdom wasn't "from this world" (18:36), Pilate was baffled. He couldn't fathom such a kingdom. Pilate's very identity was bound up with worldly symbols of success that told him who he was. Because he wore designer clothes and sported the emperor's ring on his finger, he thought he was somebody. By contrast, the gaunt Galilean standing before him appeared an abysmal failure by Pilate's standards. The man was poorly dressed, had no assets, and had lost his following. Whatever kingdom this Jesus represented, Pilate was singularly unimpressed.

Erma Bombeck wrote a book about children's experiences with cancer. In one story she told about Christina, a little girl suffering from a deadly strain of leukemia. A friend asked Christina what she would like for her eighth birthday. Christina rubbed her bald head and then rested her face in her hands. "I don't know," she answered. "I have two sticker books and a Cabbage Patch doll. I have everything."[2]

---

1 Jesus' parable of the sower (Mark 4:1-20) seeks to explain why some respond to the truth of the gospel while others do not.

2 *Proclaim*, October-December 1994, 29.

Pilate knew nothing about such a contentment that springs from the heart. Like all petty men, he was nothing without his symbols of success and status. Thus, the kingdom of God in Jesus, which began with a renewal from within (John 3:3-6), meant nothing to him. Is it any wonder that according to tradition, Pilate committed suicide? For like so many who spend their lives clawing after rank and station, he was never content. The hungers that drove him could never be satisfied.

Because he had no spiritual center, Pilate lacked a moral center also. Thus, when faced with the gravest test of his career, he bowed to public pressure. Though quickly discerning that Jesus was innocent, he feared that political unrest in his little corner of the empire might cost him his job. So after a few face-saving gestures, he caved in to the mob.

When Eisenhower's advisors were divided over whether to proceed with the D-Day invasion, the general left the room and scribbled a telegram: "Allied forces attempted a landing today in Normandy and were repulsed with heavy losses. The full responsibility for that decision rests on my shoulders alone."

If the invasion of France turned into a tragic failure, Eisenhower was prepared to take the blame. It was in part such raw courage on the part of their commander that inspired the troops to victory.[3]

Great leaders are like that: they are driven by an inner sense of conviction and not by catering to popular opinion. But Pilate had no moral compass to guide him. He wasn't a political *leader*; he was a political *animal*. The fear of losing his rank and station so terrorized him, he was easily blackmailed. So when someone cried, "If you release this man, you are no friend of the emperor" (19:12), Pilate's blood ran cold. Indeed, it appears that that thinly veiled threat sealed Jesus' fate, for within minutes of hearing it, Pilate sentenced Jesus to die.[4]

---

[3] Edwin H. Friedman, *Generation to Generation: Family Process in Church and Synagogue* (New York: Guilford Press, 1985), 237.

[4] The charge that Jesus was claiming a title usually reserved for the emperor—"Son of God" (19:7)—alarmed Pilate. In the end it was Pilate's fear that he might be charged with political disloyalty that led him to crucify Jesus (19:12-13).

Pilate's story reveals the tragic consequences of buying peace at the expense of the truth. It is such a sweet temptation. But every time we bite into that forbidden fruit, poison seeps into our soul. Any peace bought at the cost of the truth always brings tragic consequences in its wake. The abused wife accepts her husband's promises of reform, knowing full well it is only a matter of time until he strikes again. But because she doesn't know who she is without him, she can't bear to face the truth.

Likewise, distraught parents accept their teenager's lame excuse for the marijuana found in his room because they're too afraid to face the terrifying possibilities. A family or church coddles a chronic troublemaker because they lack the moral courage to put a stop to his antics. When will we learn that buying peace at the expense of the truth is always a bargain with the devil? For sooner or later, the truth comes out anyway, and all the pain our lies were supposed to save is only multiplied a thousandfold.

Those who perpetually avoid conflict thinking it is the "Christian thing to do" are sorely mistaken. We would do well to remember that our Lord was crucified by a peacemonger par excellence just trying to keep his constituents happy.

It is sometimes argued that the Gospel writers rehabilitated Pilate's image, preferring to pin responsibility for Jesus' crucifixion on the Jews. Well, if that is so, they certainly didn't do a very good job of it. Particularly in John's Gospel, if the Pilate we see is a rehabilitated figure, then the author of this work isn't much of a spin meister.[5] No, by any fair reading, Pilate comes off as a pathetic little man who couldn't summon the courage to do what in his heart he knew he needed to do. And to think that in his day he was a leading citizen of the world's greatest empire, one of the best and brightest the "kingdoms of this world" could produce!

What if we recognize more of ourselves in Pilate than we care to admit? What if we also lack a spiritual and moral center, making us a shell of the people we want to be? Where might we begin the journey toward wholeness?

---

5 See N. T. Wright, *Jesus and the Victory of God* (Philadelphia: Fortress, 1996), 544ff.

We might begin by listening to Jesus at the very point Pilate swelled with cynicism and contempt. For even amid all Pilate's maneuvering and posturing, Jesus tried to reach Pilate. He threw a line to him as one throws a life preserver to a drowning man. "Everyone who knows the truth listens to me," said Jesus (18:37).

But Pilate wasn't one to complicate his life with the truth. "Truth?" he sneered. "What's that?" Then he waved Jesus aside and started calculating his options.

What if Pilate had listened to Jesus? What was the truth he might have heard? What was the truth Jesus came into the world to proclaim and embody?

The truth was and is this: we are children of God, and God loves us with a fierce, undying love. But in letting others tell us who we are, we have lost our way. We have lost touch with our spiritual center, and like E.T. lost in an alien world, we yearn for home.

Seeing our lostness and our confusion, God sent the only Son to awaken us to our destiny forgotten. That Son—Jesus Christ—came bearing witness to the truth, the truth that God the Father holds his children precious and there is absolutely nothing we can or must do to earn that love. It is sheer gift, for it springs not from our goodness, but from the goodness of God.

All our achievements, trophies, and social climbing can never fill the emptiness within, because that empty place was instilled at creation to awaken us to our need for our Creator. It is a hunger only the very life and love of God can fill.

A little girl was watching her mother pour hot liquid into gelatin molds of various shapes. Seeing that each dessert would have its own unique pattern, she expressed her amazement by saying, "Oh, Mother! It fits them all!"

Through faith in Jesus Christ, God's living presence becomes the radiant center of a life reborn: "For God so loved the world that he gave his only Son, so that everyone who believes in him may not perish but may have eternal life" (John 3:16). That's the truth Pilate missed. But for us it is a truth yet pregnant with possibilities and promise.

Late in life, missionary evangelist E. Stanley Jones suffered a massive stroke. Despite the great effort required, he continued his ministry of writing. In his last book, *The Divine Yes*, he wrote about a Methodist bishop who had come seeking his counsel. This bishop had recently retired and had found life out of the spotlight hardly worth living. He wanted to know the secret of Jones's incredible calm even in the face of a disabling stroke.

"I told him," wrote Jones, "the difference was in giving up the innermost self to Jesus.

> The difference was in the texture of the things that held him. When the outer strands were broken by retirement, the inner strands were not enough to hold him. . . . Fortunately, with me, surrender to Jesus was the primary thing, and when the outer strands were cut by this stroke, my life didn't shake.[6]

Those who orchestrated Jesus' death, were right about *one* thing: he did sound a revolutionary call—not in the way his enemies charged and a fickle Pilate feared, but in a far more revolutionary way than they ever imagined. To confess Jesus as Lord means to take your cues from no one else. And to live in union with him is to know in the depths of your being that God already loves you as you are. So there's nothing left to prove and no need to pretend. There's just the incredible opportunity to grow in God's grace and blossom into the one and only you. Really believe that, and at long last you will be free,[7] for never again will you need somebody else to tell you who you are.

Poet e. e. cummings wrote, "To be nobody but yourself, in a world that is doing its best night and day to make you everybody else, means to fight the hardest battle any human being can fight, and never stop fighting."[8]

You don't have to fight that battle alone. Jesus Christ can help. Let him make you into a person of character and courage

---

6 E. Stanley Jones, *The Divine Yes* (Nashville: Abingdon, 1975), 63.

7 "And you will know the truth, and the truth will make you free" (John 8:32).

8 Quoted in a sermon entitled "Being What We Were Meant to Be" by John Claypool at Northminster Baptist Church, Jackson, Mississippi, April, 12, 1981.

and strength. Then at last you'll understand why the kingdom of God in Jesus really is "out of this world"!

Forgive us, O God, for our willingness
to sell your truth—and ourselves—short
in a misguided bid to appease or to please.
Rather, give us open, attentive hearts
to listen to Jesus so that his truth can set us free.
In his name we pray; help us so to live.
Amen.

Questions for Reflection

1. Jesus' comment, "My kingdom is not *of* (KJV; NRSV *from*) this world" (18:36), is sometimes taken to mean that Christianity and politics don't mix. Do you agree? What does Jesus' trial before Pilate suggest about the proper relationship between these two "kingdoms"?
2. Do you know people like Pilate who are unmoved and apathetic in the face of Jesus' truth? What would it take to reach such persons with the gospel?
3. How does Jesus' parable of the sower (Mark 4:1-20) illuminate Pilate's reaction to Jesus? Consider especially the seed that fell on the "path" (vv. 4,15).
4. Like Pilate, many of us are quite willing to buy "peace" at the expense of the truth. What does that suggest about our own spiritual and moral center?
5. Jesus' said, "For those who want to save their life will lose it, and those who lose their life for my sake will save it. What does it profit them if they gain the whole world, but lose or forfeit themselves?" (Luke 9:24-25). In what ways is the story of Pilate a dramatic restatement of this vital truth?
6. Pilate caved in to political pressures that blinded him to God's truth in Jesus. What contemporary pressures might have the same effect today?

CHAPTER 16

A Strange Kind of Glory

John 19:16-30

In Atlanta there is a knotty convergence of roads and highways the locals call "Spaghetti Junction." Anyone traveling through the area will soon discover why: along with two major highways, a number of smaller roads and cloverleafs meet to create a vast labyrinth of traffic. In fact, leaving the Atlanta perimeter and heading onto I-85 north, the access ramp rises so high over the many roads nested below, it feels as though one is piloting a small aircraft leaving the runway.

Jesus died at a sort of cosmic Spaghetti Junction. A number of factors converged to issue in his death. At one level he died because he was betrayed by a friend. At another level he died because he exposed the decaying foundation of a corrupt religious establishment. At still another level he died because the state feared his growing political clout.

Thus, the roads leading to his cross ran through the treacherous heart of a traitor, the greedy hearts of the Pharisees, and the cowardly, fear-crazed heart of a bureaucrat. His crucifixion had personal, religious, and political dimensions.

However, none of these is the focus of John's story of the cross. He in no way discounts the sordid tale of Jesus' betrayal, rigged trial, and shameful death, but these are the dark, somber tones on his canvas against which shines a stabbing light. For John, the Christ lifted high on his cross radiates a strange kind of glory.

In fact, John has recorded the phrase "lifted up" three times in his Gospel to prepare us for just this moment. "As Moses *lifted up* the serpent in the wilderness, so must the Son of Man be lifted up" (3:14). Thus, Jesus' cross is to be a source of forgiveness and new life. Then during one of his cat fights with the Pharisees, Jesus sounded the alarm again: "When you have *lifted up* the Son of Man, then you will realize that I am he" (8:28). And at the continental divide of this Gospel, as Jesus turned toward his cross, he said, "I, when I am *lifted up* from the earth, will draw all people to myself" (12:32).

"Lifted up" is John's language; it is found nowhere else in the New Testament. For him it is the language of enthronement: Jesus reigns from his cross. There he wins the world not through a coercive use of power, but through a shattering revelation of love. Ironically, the glory of the God encountering us in Jesus Christ is revealed most decisively atop Golgotha's ugly hill.[1]

Precisely because he has foreshadowed the cross throughout his Gospel, John can relate the actual event with stunning simplicity. He begins with the terse sentence, "Then [Pilate] handed him over to them to be crucified" (19:16). But for anyone who has followed the story up to this point, that stark statement is pregnant with meaning. For here the holy Son of God is condemned to die by a spineless statesman working in collusion with a corrupt religious establishment. Those eager in our own day to see the Church march to the altar with the state should take notice: Jesus died at the hands of a religious-political coalition convinced it alone could see the truth.

In its vicious assault on Jesus, this religious-political coalition actually reveals the dreadful truth of the human situation: men and women are so blinded by their selfishness, pride, and sin, they can't see the Truth, even when he is staring them in the face. Pilate speaks for all the players in this drama when he looks at Jesus blankly and asks, "What is truth?" (18:38).

---

[1] Closely related to the theme of Jesus being "lifted up" is the theme of "glory": "The hour has come for the Son of Man to be *glorified*" (12:23). The glory of God revealed first in Jesus' life (1:14; 2:11) becomes more radiant still in his death (13:31-32; 17:1) and resurrection (7:39; 17:5).

Furthermore, the bright light of God's Son coming into the world put the world's darkness into bold relief (1:9-11). Eyes accustomed to the dark found that light irritating and bothersome. The response of a fallen race was not to welcome the light, but to flee it like nocturnal creatures fleeing the dawn— and failing that, to extinguish the Christ light that stung the eyes and seared the heart. Or as John says it, "This is the judgment, that the light has come into the world, and people loved darkness rather than light because their deeds were evil" (3:19).

Judas, the Pharisees, and Pilate were not the last to resist Jesus' challenge. It is an art most of us know instinctively and well.

Some years ago during clinical training, I became fast friends with a Church of the Brethren pastor. While the rest of us budding clergy wore oxford shirts and navy blazers, he always showed up in a flannel shirt and blue jeans. Bearded and a burly six-foot-four, he looked more like a lumberjack than a preacher. I was drawn to his rugged individualism; I liked the way he challenged my rather conventional view of the world.

One of the issues we went round and round about was his commitment to pacifism. As a member of the Church of the Brethren, he believed it was wrong for a Christian to take up arms in defense of his country or for any other reason. I thought that hopelessly naive in a world where evil left unchecked grows like a malignancy.

One day after a particularly long theological bull session, I grew exasperated with what I considered his starry-eyed idealism. Weary of his endless rhetoric about turning the other cheek, I struck out at him: "Talk of 'turning the other cheek' is well and good where others are committed to that ethic, but it just won't wash in a world where the law of the jungle holds sway. What does your sentimental gospel of love and brotherhood have to do with the *real* world in which we live?"

He looked at me with a face etched by bewilderment and pain. "Everything," he answered softly, "*everything!*"

Maybe it was because with that beard he looked like a storybook Jesus, but I will never forget that look of betrayal and hurt in his eyes; and through the mist I caught sight of Golgotha's hill.

That's the terrible thing about the story of Jesus' cross. It's not just a story about the long-ago and far-away. It's also about the here and now. It's about all the ways we continue to resist Jesus' truth and try to make him into to a nice, banal prophet of middle-class morality. In Jesus' pain on the cross, we see writ large the pain we inflict on ourselves, on one another, and yes, even God, as we prefer the darkness of our lies to the liberating light of God's love.

Thus, the cross of Jesus was first of all a *judgment*. Jesus said as Golgotha loomed near, "Now is the *judgment* of this world" (12:31). The cross was the desperate, defiant act of a world shrouded in darkness to destroy Jesus and extinguish his light. The fact that they—and *we*—were and are capable of such an atrocity shows the terrifying depths of human bondage.

Of course, the cross was much more than just a revelation of the human capacity for duplicity and chilling evil. If it were that only, it would simply stand alongside Dachau and Dallas, My Lai and Memphis—to name a few. It might be different in *degree* but not in *kind* from other such killing grounds of the human spirit.

But what makes the cross radically different from every other martyrdom, ancient and modern, is *who died there*, for Jesus was no hapless martyr struck down by evil.[2] Rather, he was the Son of God going to the very depths of human depravity and sin, and dying there in holy, atoning love. Thus, his cross became forever after the sign that God knows the depths of our treachery, bondage, and shame, and loves us still.

Did not Jesus say, "No one has greater love than this, to lay down one's life for one's friends" (15:13)? At the time, it sounded like a general observation about human nature. It wasn't. It was a foreshadowing of the terrible cost his love would demand. He promised the Father—and he promised himself—that he would love his disciples "to the end" (13:1). And at the cost of his own life, that is what he did. He loved

---

[2] "No one takes my [life] from me, but I lay it down of my own accord" (John 10:18).

them even to the utter end of their betrayal, treachery, and shame.

Among mountain climbers, I'm told, the most important climber is the one holding the rope. For when a climber slips and falls, only the person holding the safety rope can save the victim. Often, as a spiraling tether shoots through the anchor's hands, it burns through his or her gloves and into the flesh. It takes consummate courage to hold on in the face of such pain. But many a falling victim has been saved because at great cost to himself or herself, the point person wouldn't let go.[3]

To the gawking crowd gathered atop Golgotha's hill, it appeared that Jesus was the victim. How could they know he was the rope man? As John's Gospel makes plain, Jesus, the holy Son of God, held the fate of a fallen world in his hands.[4] When the world's rejection and sin tore open his flesh and broke his heart, he refused to save himself. Instead, he clung to his disciples, his detractors, and his most vicious enemies with a fierce, determined love, so that someday all who looked to him in faith and longing would see revealed in his sacrifice a love that would not let them go.

Thus, the cross means that God knows the truth about us and *loves us still*. The cross means that God knows our deepest secrets and our darkest shames and *loves us still*. The cross means that God has already descended into the depths of our darkness and *loves us still*. Such love is very different from the sentimental indulgence of moral failure that passes for love in our culture; rather, this is an honest, wounded love that confronts us with the terrible cost of our infidelities but *loves us still*. Is it any wonder that when Christians look to the cross of Christ, they lift high their voices and sing, "O Love That Wilt Not Let Me Go"?[5]

So it is that Jesus dies at the intersection of the truth about the world—it is in bondage to sin—and the truth about God—

---

3 *Dynamic Preaching*, Volume 9, No. 2 (February 1994), 30.

4 "And what should I say—'Father, save me from this hour'? No, it is for this reason that I have come to this hour" (12:27).

5 Text by George Matheson, 1882. Tune: ST. MARGARET, Albert L. Peace, 1884.

that at incalculable cost, God is determined to love the world no matter what. This is the ultimate revelation of the glory of God in Jesus Christ, the glory of a holy, sacrificial, atoning love.[6] The point John wants desperately for his readers to see is that while Jesus may appear to be a condemned criminal at the mercy of the authorities, in reality he is the King of Glory reigning from his cross. Ironically, Pilate's mocking statement is true: Jesus *is* King of the Jews, the Greeks, the Romans, and the world.[7]

Jesus' lordship is revealed in his commanding presence at the trial before Pilate (18:28–19:16), in his bearing the cross alone,[8] in his touching concern for his mother (19:25-27), in his attention to fulfilling Scripture (19:28), and in his triumphant cry at his death: "It is finished!" (19:30).

But the central clue to the cosmic significance of Jesus' death is this: John portrays him as the Passover Lamb whose blood brings deliverance.[9] This is an association many modern Christians do not find endearing, but one cannot fathom John's understanding of the cross without it.

After all, the opening salvo of John's Gospel is John the Baptist's cry, "Here is the Lamb of God who takes away the sin of the world!" (1:29, 35). Later, as John's story draws to a close, he is careful to note Jesus is condemned to die at the very hour the lambs for Passover are slain (19:14; cf. 18:28).[10] Further, Jesus is handed the wine-soaked sponge on a branch of *hyssop*, not just any old "stick" (Matthew 27:48); hyssop was the small, leafy plant used to apply the blood of the Passover Lamb to the

---

[6] "Father, the hour has come; glorify your Son so that the Son may glorify you" (John 17:1).

[7] The inscription atop Jesus' cross was written in three languages representing the whole of the known world.

[8] There is no mention of Simon of Cyrene as in the other Gospels (Matthew 27:32; Mark 15:21; Luke 23:26). It was not John's intent to deny Simon's role, but rather to stress Jesus' initiative in offering up his life.

[9] For the story of the Passover Lamb, see Exodus 12:21-32.

[10] In the other Gospels, Jesus dies on the Day of Passover; in John, he dies the day before—the "Day of Preparation." In keeping with the poetic license that marks his work, it appears John has placed the crucifixion a day earlier so it coincides with the slaughter of the Passover lambs.

door frame (Exodus 12:22). And finally, John notes that none of Jesus' bones were broken, "that the scripture might be fulfilled" (19:32-33, 36). What Scripture? The Scripture that prescribed no bone of the Passover Lamb be broken (Exodus 12:46).

The modern reader might ask, "So what? What does all that have to do with my life today? If John wanted to use ghoulish imagery drawn from of an ancient religious festival, so be it. I'll fashion images of my own."

Good. Have at it. Every generation needs to retell the gospel story in the language and idioms of its age. But first we must plumb the terrifying depths of the original story in all of its ugliness, wretchedness, and pain. Those who actually lived through the horror of Jesus' betrayal, trial, and death never ceased to wonder that their Lord's blood flowed for *them*. They shuddered to realize it cost God that much to take hold of a wounded, rabid world and pull it to safety.

Writer Annie Dillard tells the remarkable story of an Eskimo mother stranded with her daughter in the Arctic. The two of them were left after everyone else starved to death during an unusually severe winter. In search of food and help, the woman wandered with her baby until she came to an abandoned camp by a lake. There she found a fishing pole, line, and one small fishhook.

But there was no bait and no hope of bait. Then the baby cried in hunger and distress. Her heart breaking, the mother took a knife and cut a strip of flesh from her own thigh. Using that worm of flesh, she caught a fish. And after feeding the baby and herself, she used the fish gut for bait.

So it was that she and the child survived that terrible winter. In the spring she walked out of the wilderness carrying her child. On her thigh she forevermore had a scar showing the cost of their salvation.[11]

Dare we say it? The cross is an ugly scar on the thigh of God. It is the jagged shape of holy love sprawled atop Golgotha's hill. It is a dreadful reminder of what it cost to save this broken world.

---

[11] Annie Dillard, *The Writing Life* (New York: Harper & Row, 1989), 12-13.

This was not some arbitrary "cost" paid by a loving Son to a vengeful Father. The twisted notion that Jesus died to appease or "buy off" God's avenging wrath is a diabolical distortion of Holy Scripture.[12] No, the cross was simply what it cost to expose the toxic effects of human sinfulness and the uncharted depths of the love of God. At the intersection of those two—the horizontal and vertical beams of his cross, if you will—Jesus Christ died. And from the wounded heart of God flowed the salvation of the world: "For *God* so loved the world, that he gave his only begotten Son, that whosoever believeth in him should not perish, but have everlasting life" (John 3:16, KJV).

Yes, it is a strange kind of glory, a glory marking the descent from the dizzying heights of the Godhead (John 1) to the dizzying depths of human depravity and sin (John 19). To be sure, it is not the glory of dazzling grandeur; it is instead the glory of a dazzling grace. For the Christ who dwelt among us in the flesh (1:14) has dwelt among us even unto death. When he comes to us in the wake of his Easter rising, he yet bears the wounds of his bloody engagement with a broken world (20:24-27).

Little wonder Jesus cried from his cross, "It is finished!" There is nothing more God can do to reveal the depths of his love: "Christ, our Passover lamb, has been sacrificed" (1 Corinthians 5:7, NIV).

With heads bowed in adoration and awe, we cry, "Alleluia. Let us keep the feast!"

Lord Jesus Christ, meet us at the intersection
of our great need and your great love.
Cast out our fear and shame by the power
of a grace greater than all our sin.
Be the light that shatters our darkness

---

[12] A text often cited in defense of this position is "My God, my God, why have you forsaken me?" (Mark 15:34). But that passage is better understood as expressing the human dimension of Jesus' struggle on earth than the attitude of God in heaven. The notion that God the Father could ever turn away from God the Son is especially untenable in John's Gospel; in this Gospel they are always one in the bond of God the Holy Spirit.

and the love that makes it safe to come out of hiding.
In your name, we pray, O crucified and risen One,
Amen.

Questions for Reflection

1. Is it possible to have a vital Christian faith while ignoring or minimizing the meaning of the cross? Why or why not?
2. The New Testament uses a wide variety of word pictures to reveal the significance of Christ's death. Among these are ransom (Mark 10:45), redemption (Colossians 1:14), peace with God (Romans 5:1), God for us (Romans 8:31ff.), sacrifice (Hebrews 9:26), and reconciliation (Ephesians 2:16). Which of these concepts do you prefer? Why? Consider using a concordance (an index to the words in the Bible) to trace that word or concept throughout Scripture.
3. Can you remember a time when you felt really loved, even in the face of some great failure or shame? How might that experience illuminate the meaning of Jesus' death?
4. Can you suggest other images or ideas from contemporary experience that might illustrate the significance of the cross?
5. In the prologue to John's Gospel, Jesus is said to be the one who brings both grace and truth (1:14, 17). How do these two qualities come together at his cross?
6. In John's Gospel, Jesus is both the Good Shepherd who gives his life for the sheep (10:11), an active image, and the Lamb of God slain for the sins of the world (1:29, 36), a passive image. How do you relate these seemingly contradictory facets of his death on the cross?
7. How are Jesus' disciples to reflect and embody his radical brand of sacrificial love? See Luke 9:23; John 15:12-14; Galatians 2:20.

CHAPTER 17

Seeing Easter through Our Tears

John 20:1-18

Do you remember the worst day of your life?

Maybe it was the day your mother died, and your tether to ages past was gone; suddenly you felt adrift in the universe, all alone.

Or maybe it was the day the divorce papers were signed, and you saw in the permanence of that silky black ink the terrible finality of it all.

Perhaps the worst day came when corporate downsizing leaped off the pages of *Newsweek* and became a personal life crisis. Suddenly all your carefully crafted dreams were snatched away by a cruel stroke of fate.

The worst day of Mary of Magdala's life was the day Jesus died—not just because of the abject horror of the scene, but because when he died, everything in her life that mattered died with him.

While vital and alive, Jesus had cast seven demons from her soul.[1] Now that he was gone, she felt the old psychosis nibbling at her brain like a rat chewing through a wall. It was only a matter of time until the demons had their way with her once again.

---

[1] Cf. Mark 16:9; Luke 8:2.

144

Still, with the remnants of sanity and courage remaining, Mary wanted to accompany the other women to the tomb that fateful Sunday morning. Joseph of Arimathea and Nicodemus tried to give Jesus a proper burial; but it was a frantic, rushed job, and frankly, some things just need a woman's touch. So the determined little band set out in the wee hours of the morning, while it was still dark.

When the women reached the tomb, they discovered that someone had rolled back the stone that had sealed the grave. Perhaps some of the men, anticipating their errand of mercy, had performed that difficult chore. But when the women raised their torch and looked inside, they saw that the body was gone. And then the sickening realization hit home. Jesus' enemies could grant him no peace even in death. It appeared they had taken his body, planning to inflict still further indignities upon him. Mary shuddered at the thought of entering Jerusalem's square that very morning and seeing her Lord's body hanging from a post.

The women ran back to Jerusalem to sound the alarm. Rousing Peter and the beloved disciple from sleep, Mary broke the news. "They have taken the Lord from the tomb and we don't know where he is!"

Peter and the beloved disciple—traditionally thought to be John—raced to the tomb. Mary, winded and shaken, followed after them.

John, arriving first, stooped to peer cautiously into the tomb. But Peter—ever impulsive—ran right inside. In the dim morning light, both were struck by the strangeness of the scene. For there, lying on the floor, were the linen strips in which Jesus had been buried. Peter and John exchanged a puzzled glance. Why would grave robbers strip the corpse before whisking it away?

While Mary lingered outside, the beloved disciple joined Peter inside to examine the evidence up close. Not only were the burial wrappings lying there undisturbed, but the headpiece was separate from the other strips. It still stood in its folds, turban-like as it had been wound about Jesus' head. It was as though Jesus' body had vaporized, leaving the grave clothes behind like the wispy cocoon of a butterfly. Could those grave clothes be the spent wrappings from which a new life emerged?

An observation by Cecil B. De Mille speaks to that question. It was a lazy summer afternoon, and he was reading in a rowboat just off shore. Glancing down, he saw some water beetles in the water and mud below. Eventually one crawled up onto the boat, attached itself to the boat's woodwork, and died. De Mille turned back to his reading, trying to ignore the hot sun beating down on his head. He writes:

> In about three hours I noticed my water beetle again. He was parched. His back was cracking open. As I watched, out of the back of the dead beetle I saw crawling a new form. First, a moist head, then wings. Finally, a most beautiful dragonfly emerged. As I sat watching, it took to the air. It hovered over the surface just a few inches over the water beetles beneath. They did not even know it was there.[2]

While the risen Christ hovered nearby, his disciples—intent on finding a dead Jesus—didn't even notice. But now, looking back with the eyes of faith, we know the significance of those grave clothes. They were the brittle shell of death from which the risen Lord took wings. They were crisp fall leaves yielding to the coming of spring.

Incidentally, that little detail about the grave clothes has all the marks of an actual historical remembrance. If the story of Jesus' resurrection were a fabrication, who would have thought to include such a mundane observation? Yet as street smart detectives know, it is usually in the mundane details—that liars and thieves forget—that the truth comes out.

Those grave clothes are a startling sign of our Easter hope. They are a sign that our Lord vacated his tomb as surely as the smokey wisp of a snake's skin means a serpent was near.

---

[2] Quoted in unpublished sermon, April 7, 1985, entitled "The Rest of the Story," by Deryl Fleming, then pastor of the Ravensworth Baptist Church, Annandale, Virginia.

Yet they are only a sign pointing to a larger truth; they are not compelling proof in themselves. For even Peter, first on the scene, did not come to an Easter faith because of those grave clothes. Indeed, with the possible exception of the beloved disciple—whom we read *believed* when he saw those linen remnants—no one was convinced Jesus had been raised because of the empty tomb. Then as now, the fact of his empty tomb raised the *question* of Easter. But it took a life-changing encounter with the risen Lord to *answer* it.

After examining the scene, Peter and John didn't race back to Jerusalem proclaiming, "The Lord is risen!" Instead, we read simply, "Then the disciples returned to their homes" (20:10), which suggests that whatever the beloved disciple "believed" when he saw those grave clothes didn't change his life. After the disturbing events of the morning, he and Peter just went home, presumably to resume the broken lives they had left behind.

Only Mary lingered at the tomb. She had nowhere else to go. Without Jesus, she might have had a house, but she didn't have a home. She had no sanctuary, no refuge, no place to mend her broken wings. So she bowed her head and began to weep.

She wept for how beautiful life had been with Jesus and how empty it was without him. She wept at being denied the simple privilege of anointing her Lord's body and giving him a decent burial. She wept that the God whom Jesus called "Father" turned out to be an inept, abusive parent like the one she had known as a child. Shaking with remorse and sadness, Mary wept. Soon the ground outside the empty tomb was pocked by tears marking the spot where, for her, life had ended.

Finally, peering through her tears, Mary peeked once more into the tomb. This time she saw something Peter and John had not seen; she saw two angels sitting in the tomb. "Woman, why are you weeping?" they asked her.

Then she answered for all those who have lost Jesus and who, in losing him, have lost themselves: "They have taken away my Lord, and I do not know where they have laid him" (20:13).

I lost Jesus once. It was in college when I learned that the Bible was not a verbatim transcript of the musings of God, but a very human testimony to a more than human Word. For me that was a terribly unsettling experience. How could I trust a book so very human and yet divine? What if the Gospels were just religious short stories with no basis in fact, no pinnings in history to anchor their truth? What if the empty tomb was the figment of a pious imagination and not the actual remembrance of disheveled disciples, who—when they first saw it—shook their heads in disbelief?

During that period of disorientation and doubt, the Jesus I had known as a child was snatched away. Suddenly the radiant center of my life was gone, and I felt empty, adrift, and all alone. Instinctively, in the depths of my being, I knew the anguish of Mary's cry: "They have taken away my Lord, and I do not know where they have laid him!"

Have you ever lost Jesus and wondered if talk of his resurrection was—as his disciples first put it—an "idle tale"? (Luke 24:11). Have the dark clouds of despair ever shut out his light? Has some fearsome storm of discontent robbed you of him even now?

If so, then follow your tears to Easter. After all, it was Mary's weeping that opened her eyes to the risen Christ. Peter and John looked at the evidence, such as it was, dusted off their robes, and headed for home. But Mary stood outside that tomb, honoring her grief, until at long last she saw Easter through her tears.

What was it the angel asked her? "Why are you *weeping?*" (20:13). And what did Jesus say when first she turned to him, not yet knowing who he was: "Why are you *weeping?* Whom are you looking for?" (20:15).

When I lost Jesus, it wasn't an empty tomb that led me back to him; it was an empty heart. Without him, my life, like Mary's, came crashing down. And I discovered with George MacDonald that "I would rather die forevermore believing as Jesus believed, than live forevermore believing as those who deny him."[3]

---

[3] Quoted in Ronald Heim's, *George MacDonald: Victorian Mythmaker* (Nashville: Star Song, 1993), xvii.

Mary honored her tears. With a fierce, determined honesty, she stared point blank at the barrenness of a life without Jesus. Is it any wonder she was crying?

But by the grace of God, Mary's tears were not the end of the story. Easter happened when she saw Jesus through her tears. At first, caught up in her grief, she mistook him for the gardener. Through her sniffles, she blurted, "Sir, if you have carried him away, tell me where you have laid him, and I will take him away" (20:15).

Jesus reached up and gently wiped at her tears. "*Mary!*" he said emphatically, as he had called her name when casting out her demons.

Suddenly, recognition dawned. "Rabbouni!" she gasped (v. 16).[4] Then she reached for him and let her crumpled frame fall into his arms.

And so it was for me when at last Jesus found me on the far side of my tears. Pointing an angry, accusing finger at the heavens, I cried to an absent, uncaring God, "They have taken my Lord, and I don't know where they have laid him!"

And then, in the wake of that terrible wail, there was an awful, dead silence—until in the quietness of a broken heart, I heard Jesus call my name: "*Bobby.*" Although I couldn't see the Master, I never doubted it was he, for in the meeting of our hearts, the light of Easter shone. And in the mystery of his living presence, my fractured selfhood found healing and a great calm took command of my soul.

E. Stanley Jones, the famed missionary to India, told of visiting the Mosque of Saint Sophia in Istanbul. This mosque, located in a former Christian center, was built over the ruins of a church. All the Christian symbols were destroyed and Arabic architecture and markings put in their place.

One day as Jones craned his neck, looking up into the building's dome, he grabbed a companion by the sleeve and cried, "Look! He's coming back!" For through the decaying plaster and paint of untold centuries, an image of the ascending

---

4 As John takes care to tell us, *Rabbouni* means "teacher."

Christ was becoming visible. "You can't wipe him out!" the great evangelist exclaimed. "He keeps coming back!"[5]

That's the thing about Jesus. Nail him up and write him off, but he keeps coming back. Consign him to some tomb of disbelief, but he keeps coming back. Through all our doubts and fears, and supremely, through our tears, he keeps coming back!

Time and time again we have left Jesus for dead in some graveyard of our own despair, then in the quietness of a broken heart, he called *our* names. And in the crucible of our own experience, Easter happened!

Granted, Jesus doesn't always come back exactly as we have known him before. Each time he reclaims us, we gain a deeper apprehension of his mystery, majesty, and love. As he said to Mary, so he says to us, "Don't cling to the old me. Let my grace and glory shine ever new."

Through all the struggles and sorrows of this mortal life, Jesus keeps coming back and surprising us by whatever empty tomb last tried to hold him. Whether we understand a little or a lot, this we confess: a life we took for over found new wings because of Jesus. And the one whom others revere as a great teacher only, we know to be a living Lord.

In the *Oxford Book of Prayer,* George Appleton makes this lovely offering:

> O Christ, my Lord, again and again I have said with Mary Magdalene, "They have taken away my Lord and I know not where they have laid him." I have been desolate and alone. And thou hast found me again, and I know that what hast died is not thou, my Lord, but only my idea of thee, the image which I have made to preserve what I have found, and to be my security.
>
> I shall make another image, O Lord, better than the last. That too must go, and all successive images, until I

---

5 E. Stanley Jones, "Christ Is the Answer," in G. Paul Butter, ed., *Best Sermons: 1955 Edition* (New York: McGraw-Hill, 1955), 54.

come to the blessed vision of thyself, O Christ, my Lord.[6]

If you've lost sight of Jesus, try looking for him through your tears. In the end, Mary found him where she had found him at the beginning: in the midst of her pain and in the ache of his absence. That just may be where the living Christ is waiting to meet you, even now.

Lord Jesus Christ, burst free of every tomb
where we would leave you lay. Amid all our doubts,
bewilderment, and tears, keep surprising us
with the miracle of your life.
Turn every graveyard we thought was the end
into a new beginning. In your name we pray
and hope to live.
Amen.

Questions for Reflection

1. Jesus' first resurrection appearance in John's Gospel is to Mary. This is the last of many occasions in this Gospel where women appear at strategic points: 2:1-11, 4:1-42, 11:20-44, 12:1-8, 19:25-27, and 20:1-18. What does this suggest about the role of women in the Church of John's day? In our day?
2. What is the importance of the empty tomb in John's narrative? Since it was the appearances of the risen Lord that ignited the Easter faith of the disciples, does that mean the empty tomb does not matter? If not, why did the Gospel writers report it in such detail? See 1 Corinthians 15:3-28.
3. Easter is often likened to the renewal of spring or a rebirth of hope. Are these adequate expressions of the Church's Easter proclamation? Why or why not?

---

6 George Appleton, *The Oxford Book of Prayer* (New York: Oxford University Press, 1985), 147.

4. Can you remember a time when Mary's confession became your own: "They have taken my Lord and I don't know where to find him!" What got you through that difficult ordeal? Or are you standing outside the empty tomb weeping even now?

5. Mary saw Jesus in a visible manifestation of his Easter glory. Believers today can only "see" him by faith. Is such an experience of his risen presence, while very different, any less real? See John 20:29 and 1 Peter 1:8-9.

CHAPTER 18

On Behalf of
Believing Thomas

John 20:19-30

According to the legend of the Australian thornbird, the moment a thornbird leaves its nest, it goes in search of a thorn tree. When it finds one, the bird nosedives into the tree's thorny branches. Then as the bird slowly perishes, it lifts up a song considered even lovelier than the nightingale's. Out of the thornbird's agony comes its greatest song.

Thomas is the thornbird of the Fourth Gospel. For out of the terrible agony of his defection and doubt came faith's sweetest song: "My Lord and my God!" (20:28). Indeed, with Thomas's confession, the Gospel of John comes full circle, ending where it began: "In the beginning was the Word, and the Word was with God, and the Word *was* God" (1:1).

Yet Thomas is remembered not as a person of faith, but as "the doubter." The sting of his bitter words—"Unless I see the mark of the nails in his hands, and put my finger in the mark of the nails and my hand in his side, I will not believe" (20:25)—remained etched in the memory of many. But that painful moment in Thomas's spiritual pilgrimage was not his stopping point. In fact, when at last he discovered for *himself* that Jesus was alive, his faith was stronger for the doubt that had preceded it. The finished steel of his confession was forged in the heart of an honest man who would not feign a faith he did not feel.

153

While Thomas is the disciple remembered as "the doubter," he was hardly alone in that. All the disciples experienced the horror of soul-numbing, faith-crushing doubt. The death of Jesus put a huge question mark in front of everything they believed. Luke tells us that *all* the disciples dismissed the women's report of the resurrection as "an idle tale" (Luke 24:11). So far as they could see, Jesus' death meant the end. Death had always meant the end before. Thus, Thomas was hardly the only doubter in the crowd. His only crime was being absent that first Easter eve when Jesus appeared to his disciples in Jerusalem (20:19-24). Consequently, he missed having his faith reignited by that encounter with the risen Lord.

As to why Thomas was absent, we can only guess. From what little we see of Thomas in John's Gospel, he appears a rugged individualist. So when his world came crashing down, he was the type who had to find his way alone.

For example, after Jesus told his disciples that he was going away to prepare a place for them, he added the aside, "And you know the way to the place where I am going" (John 14:4). The others nodded like they knew what Jesus was talking about. Thomas alone popped off with the frank admission, "Lord, the truth is, we don't have a clue where you're going. So how can we know the way?"

Only then did Jesus deliver the gem for which we have Thomas to thank, "*I* am the way, the truth, and the life. No one comes to the Father but by me."

On another occasion, Jesus decided to return to the vicinity of Jerusalem in the wake of Lazarus's death. Knowing Jesus' enemies had a price on his head, the disciples feared such a move courted confrontation and even death. But Thomas cheered the frightened band with his brave pronouncement, "Let us also go, that we may die with him" (John 11:16).

Thus, from the quick snapshots we see of Thomas in the Fourth Gospel,[1] Thomas emerges as a man of conviction and courage. He was prepared to die with Jesus; he just couldn't

---

[1] In the first three Gospels, Thomas is mentioned by name, but his portrait is not developed.

bear the prospect of living without him. So as his fellow disciples huddled in the upper room, cowering behind locked doors, Thomas—never a company man—chose to go it alone. He was probably out wandering the hillsides, wracking his brain and searching his heart, when the risen Lord first appeared to the disciples in Jerusalem.

There is a certain nobility about Thomas's defiance. He wasn't one to go along for the ride, so when he was greeted by ecstatic disciples crying, "We have seen the Lord! We have seen the Lord!" (20:25), that wasn't good enough for him. Thomas wasn't about to buy the party line just because others said it was so, for he knew that a faith not forged in the fire of personal experience was no faith at all.

Frankly, a little hard-nosed skepticism like Thomas's can be an invaluable asset in the life of faith. It keeps one from being victimized by charlatans and con artists. Cults, for example, thrive on the "blind faith" of their adherents. But a faith that is "blind" isn't faith at all. Faith—especially in John's Gospel—is the capacity to "see" God's truth in Jesus. And sometimes doubt is the darkness that precedes faith's dawning.

By contrast, the infamous Heaven's Gate cult demanded a suspension of all doubt. In that chilling video of the cultists cheerfully contemplating suicide, they all appeared in pairs. Why? Because each cult member was given a "check partner" to guard against independent thought. Should someone prove stubborn enough to think for himself or herself, despite such controls, that person was sent to a special "decontamination zone" for a booster shot of brainwashing. Contact with family members or anyone else who questioned the group's spin on reality was absolutely forbidden.[2]

Among many Christians, doubt is regarded with suspicion. Those who dare to question the Bible or popular Christian belief are viewed as desecrating the faith. But as the Heaven's Gate tragedy would remind us, being willing to parrot another's creed is not faith. It is conformity at best, if not outright delusion. Only those like Thomas, who refuse to buy

---

[2] Cf. Evan Thomas, et. al. "The Next Level." *Newsweek*, April 7, 1997, 32.

spiritual peace at the cost of intellectual integrity, will discover the truth that sets them free. As the great preacher Henry Drummond once wrote, "Better a little faith, dearly won, better launched alone on the infinite bewilderment of truth, than perish on the splendid plenty of the richest creeds."[3]

Some degree of doubting is probably essential if we are to take whatever faith we inherited from others and make it our own. Does that faith reflect our own understanding of Scripture and experience of God? Or like young David rattling around in King Saul's bulky armor, do we need a faith that better fits the unique contours of our life (see 1 Samuel 17:38-40)? This is something the defenders of orthodoxy always forget: a living faith doesn't come straight off the rack. Always, it must be personally tailored.

Thus, Thomas should not be condemned for his doubts, not if they were the honest protests of a broken heart. Indeed, that is something we need to learn from his story. Though he wore the scarlet D on his forehead, he still had a place among the community of believers. No one said to him, "Thomas, we're tired of your raining on our parade. We're tired of your probing questions and critical spirit. Why don't you take your doubts and go elsewhere?" Instead, when the other disciples told him of seeing the Lord in his absence, they invited Thomas to bring his doubts with him and take his place at the table. So the next time Jesus appeared, Thomas was there (20:26).

The worst thing to do when struggling with doubt is to cut oneself off from the community of faith. Had Thomas persisted in such a go-it-alone spirituality, his doubts may well have hardened into cynicism. But because he kept his doubts in creative tension with the witness of the Church, they were but a way station in his journey of faith and not a final destination.

Unfortunately, when doubt strikes, most people cut themselves off from their faith community at the very time they need it most. This is common, for example, in the young college

---

[3] As cited by Paul Brand and Philip Yancey in *Fearfully and Wonderfully Made* (Grand Rapids: Zondervan, 1980), 89.

student whose childhood faith undergoes rigorous testing at the university. At the very time his or her Christian convictions are being challenged by new teachings and lifestyles, the typical college student is inactive in a local congregation. As a consequence, the student tends to develop intellectually while his or her spiritual growth is on hold. Thus, many young people graduate from college with their childhood faith in ruins, with nothing better built in its place.

Or in the wake of a setback, tragedy, or bereavement, when doubts are circling a wounded faith like vultures, many people find it difficult to remain active in church. The church reminds them of assurances that proved shallow or prayers that weren't answered, at least as one had hoped. Yet, to drop out of church at such a time is to rob oneself of the very resource needed to keep doubt and despair from overwhelming the soul.

Somehow, Thomas had learned that lesson. For despite seeking solitude to plumb the depths of his pain, he also recognized his need for the fellowship of believers. Therefore, he was present that next Sunday evening when the disciples gathered at the appointed place and time. And no one showed him the door because he wasn't at that moment a card-carrying member of the faithful. He was welcome, despite his doubts, in the First Church of Jerusalem. May his spiritual siblings yet find a warm welcome in our churches today.

Thus, a doubting Thomas was present when the risen Christ appeared the second time. The Lord greeted his disciples as before: "Peace be with you" (20:26; cf. v. 19). Then he turned to Thomas, for it was primarily to address him that this encore appearance was arranged. "Thomas," said the Master, radiant and full of life, "Draw near and put your finger in my nail prints, and your hand in my side. It's time to put your doubts behind you and believe" (20:27).

Such encouragement in the struggle to believe is a sign of our risen Lord's presence. To whatever extent possible, he gives us what we need to commit ourselves to him: fellow pilgrims whose vibrant faith raises the possibility of our own; the hint of an unseen presence weaving amid surprising circumstances we just can't quite ascribe to chance; a passage from

Scripture that speaks with pointed relevance to our most pressing need. Always, Jesus is teasing us as he teased Thomas to move through our doubts in the direction of faith. For while the territory of doubt is a good place to visit, it is a terrible place to live.

As many who stayed mired too long in their doubts can attest, doubts left untended soon harden into the concrete of cynicism and despair. That's why it is so important that we bring our doubts to church, where they can be tested and challenged. As Jesus said to Thomas, so he says to us, "Don't let your doubts land you in that hellish place where there is no faith at all. Instead, in light of my risen presence now made known to you, take the risk and believe."

Thomas stood there with a quivering jaw and a broken heart. Seeing his Lord before him, he felt no need to touch the wounds. Instead, the mere sight of the risen Christ quickened his faltering faith and drove him to his knees. Overcome with wonder and awe, he cried, "My Lord and my God!" (20:28).

Jesus then asked, "Have you believed because you have seen me?" (20:29). The answer for Thomas was the same as for all the rest of the disciples: yes, he believed in the risen Lord because he saw him and glimpsed within time a hint of his eternal glory. That was, no doubt, what it took to ignite the faith of those first disciples and birth the Church.

We belong to a different place and time. We have neither seen the Jesus of history nor feasted our eyes upon the glory of the risen Christ. And so Jesus spoke words to Thomas aimed past him to us: "Have you believed because you have seen me? Blessed are those who have not seen and yet . . . believe" (20:29).

Robed in those words, the living Christ comes seeking us as he came to those first disciples who were crippled by fear and doubt. He offers us the same life-giving promise: "Peace be with you" (20:26). Though we cannot see Jesus as they did, he is no less real. For as he breathes his Spirit upon us, we experience the gentle calm of his peace (John 14:25-27). And in the warmth of his presence, the icy grip of doubt begins to melt.

During the Korean War, the U.N. forces used a certain bridge to supply troops to the front. Unfortunately, the bridge was in an area prone to flooding and often disappeared beneath the swollen river. When this happened, the drivers learned to guide their vehicles down to the edge of the river and then nudge them ever so slowly into the water at the point where the bridge ought to be. Always it was there, and throughout the war, that bridge never failed or washed away. It was ever present to support the troops that passed across it.

So it is with the living Christ. Though not visible to the naked eye, he is present still the same. And every time we venture out in faith and entrust ourselves to him, we discover his power to bear us up and bear us through. When we call his name, there is an answering presence. And our souls grow strong in the confidence that we do not traverse this mortal plane alone, for underneath are the everlasting arms. Or as 1 Peter 1:8 expresses it, "Although you have not seen him, you love him; and even though you do not see him now, you believe in him and rejoice with an indescribable and glorious joy."

We can thank Thomas for the gracious words "Blessed are those who have not seen and yet . . . believe." And we can thank him for a lot more besides. Were it not for him, we might believe those who tell us doubt is the mortal enemy of faith. Because of our brother Thomas, we know better. We know that doubt can be the midwife of a new and more vital communion with God.

Maybe Tennyson was right: "There lives more faith in honest doubt, believe me, than in half the creeds."[4] For from the depths of Thomas's doubt sprang the highest confession in John's Gospel: "My Lord and my God!" In the end he wasn't doubting Thomas at all, but *believing* Thomas.

And so it can be for us if we trust our Lord enough to bring even our doubts to him. For if he doesn't fear facing them, why should we?

Like the father of the demon possessed boy,
we cry to you, O Christ:
"I believe; help my unbelief!" [Mark 9:24].

---

4 Quoted in William Barclay, *The Gospel of John*, vol. 2, rev. ed. (Philadelphia: Westminster Press, 1975), 276.

Give us the courage to trust you even amid our doubts,
that a more mature and robust faith might be born.
Help us forge our own confession in the refining fire
of your presence and truth. In your name, we pray.
Amen.

Questions for Reflection

1. Can you remember a time when you were mired in doubt? How was the community of faith helpful—or hurtful—during the struggle?
2. Why are scapegoats like Thomas, the *doubter,* and Judas, the *betrayer,* such a fixture of human experience?
3. What periods or events in life tend to precipitate the greatest doubts? How might an awareness of this impact the Church's ministry?
4. Are doubts usually resolved by an intellectual process, a spiritual awakening, or both? What does Thomas's experience suggest?
5. Why did Thomas feel no need to touch the wounds of the risen Christ?
6. Some argue that calling Jesus one's "Lord and God" (20:28) is sheer blasphemy. Is it? Why or why not? Based on your study of John's Gospel, how would you qualify the statement, "Jesus is God"?
7. In what sense are those "who have not seen and yet have come to believe" more "blessed" than the first disciples? See John 16:7 for a hint.

CHAPTER 19

Christian Faith Is a Personal Matter

John 21:1-17

There is a lot in the Bible I don't understand and a number of strange occurrences reported there with which I have no personal experience. But when it comes to the matter related in John 21—namely, of returning from a fishing trip with no fish— I'm an expert! As one who has often headed back to the dock empty-handed, I speak with authority: the last thing a frustrated fisherman wants to hear is the question put to the disciples by the stranger on shore: "What did ya catch?"

I can see the hair bristling on Peter's thick, tanned neck as he, the master fisherman, is forced to confess, "Nothing!" The growl in his voice puts others on notice to keep their distance.

But the pesky stranger doesn't take the hint. "Try casting your net on the other side of the boat," he says, "and I bet you'll catch some."

Galled by this unsolicited advice, Peter and the others are eager to prove the meddler wrong. They do as suggested expecting to hold an empty net aloft while shouting the retort, "See, they're just not biting."

But suddenly, for the first time in a long, weary night, the net grows taunt, then heavy, as the boat is nearly capsized by a huge haul of fish. As everyone strains at the net, the beloved disciple hazards a second glance at the stranger on shore.

Suddenly recognition dawns: "It's the Lord!" he cries. Peter and the others turn to look and see Jesus crack a smile before breaking into a deep, full-bellied laugh. An instant later Peter is in the water swimming to meet his Lord, while Jesus waits to greet him with a bear hug and a charcoal-broiled breakfast.

What was it that led the beloved disciple—and then the others—to recognize they were confronted by the risen Christ? At first they didn't have a clue who he was, but suddenly their eyes were opened and they recognized the Master.

It reminds me of bumping into someone at a reunion whom I had not seen in years but recognizing the person instantly because of a certain unique expression or quirk. On another occasion, perhaps a distinctive scent indicated a loved one or friend was near, even though he or she had not been spotted. I still remember my excitement as a boy when I smelled Aqua-Velva in the house, for that meant Daddy was home. Or perhaps in a crowded restaurant a woman looks in vain for her party until the sound of a distinctive laugh calls to her like a signal beam guiding a lost plane home. People have signatures other than those penned on a page that tell us who they are.

What is Jesus' signature that tells us he is in the vicinity even when, wrapped in the morning mist, he remains hidden from view? Is it not the presence of a mysterious grace that surprises and renews us when we least expect it? Facing an uncertain future, our nets empty and our reserves depleted, suddenly the strength to go on crystallizes within us. In the midst of some great heartbreak or sorrow, a strange peace settles over our soul. In struggling with a longstanding problem, we suddenly see with clarity what we must do and know for a certainty that this time *we will do it*. In ways such as these, we find ourselves startled from time to time by hints of the divine. Rare is the person who cannot remember being touched by that mysterious power Christians call "grace."

But what makes Christian faith *Christian*, is recognizing with the beloved disciple that such surprising grace is the signature of the risen Lord. To suddenly realize "It is the Lord!" is to experience the miracle of Easter. Christians are not alone in toiling fruitlessly at the edge of their despair when suddenly, mysteriously, a moment's insight or inspiration turns hopelessness into hope. But what puts the song of Easter on a believer's lips is knowing that such grace has a name, such grace has a face: it is the calling card of Jesus Christ. It means that he is lingering in the gray, misty morning of an awakened imagination as surely as he meandered along the shoreline of the Sea of Galilee that magical morning long ago.

Some years ago, my family and I moved to Danville, Virginia. En route to this new home, our car broke down about thirty miles south of town. Due to the aid of some good Samaritans, we were eventually able to resume our journey, arriving at our new residence late that evening. Our eleven-year-old daughter, Whitney, had been riding in one of the moving trucks. Immediately upon our arrival, she went to retrieve from the car, Tiger, the family cat. But she discovered to her horror that Tiger was gone. A frantic search confirmed the worst. Apparently Tiger had slipped out of the car as it was being repaired by the road.

Surely the worst of all pains is the pain of one's child. My daughter's anguish over the loss of her pet nearly crushed my heart. And so, though the hour was late and we were exhausted, there was no question that we would go back and look for the cat, even though I felt it was a futile exercise.

As we barreled down the highway, our shaken family prayed aloud and asked God to help us find our lost and bewildered tabby. But not wanting to unduly tax the Almighty's patience or providence, I hedged my bets, being careful to pray Tiger would find a good home in the event we did not find her. With the hour nearing midnight and torrential rains pouring down, it is not hard to imagine which prayer I thought would be answered.

Finally, we arrived near the spot of the breakdown. Standing in the rain by the roadside with huge semis thundering by, we called Tiger's name into the night. As I expected, nothing happened.

Then I realized we were not at the precise spot of the breakdown. So we walked another fifty feet into the rain, our flashlight barely piercing the thick night. Once again we knelt to call for Tiger, and as we did, I heard a slight rustling to my left. Expecting to a see a possum, I turned my light toward the noise and saw cat eyes gleaming in the dark. "Tiger!" Whitney screamed as the startled cat sauntered out of the bushes to be swept up into the arms of an ecstatic child.

If ever I felt myself to be engaged in a futile fishing expedition, like those disciples of old, it was when we set out to look for that lost cat by the highway in the dead of night. And pastor or not, I never dreamed our prayers for the safe return of that cat would be answered, and on another occasion perhaps they would not. But that strange, whimsical night we knew ourselves to have been graced by the unseen Savior, whose heart like mine had been broken by a young girl's tears.

And lest the cynic, still very much alive within me, should try to chalk it all up to coincidence, a falling star marked our departure back to Danville. My wife, Bambi, saw it streak across the sky just as we were pulling away. It appeared to land directly behind us. It was as though the risen Christ had thrown in a cosmic exclamation point so even I could not miss that it was he who had met us by the side of the road.

By the roadside and by the shore, and a thousand points between, the risen Christ comes to surprise and renew us in the midst of our skepticism and empty toiling. When we grow forgetful of his presence thinking we have to do it all ourselves, he comes to remind us that we are not alone. When we know that in our own strength the challenge we face is insurmountable, he comes to steady and steel us in the power of his risen life. Exhausted and forlorn, staring hopelessly at our empty nets, we know the risen Christ has come calling when suddenly there is abundance in the face of want, peace in the face of tumult, and hope in the face of despair. And to our hearts leaps the confidence, "It is the Lord!" as we stand in awe of his grandeur and enthralled by his grace.

Perhaps some would argue that it matters not whether one knows the name of the stranger at whose word the nets fill with bounty. After all, the huge haul of fish is yours to keep in any event. Yet the joy of the catch pales in comparison to the joy of knowing Jesus. Was not Peter quick to leave his jackpot behind when he recognized the broad, beaming smile of the Master?

Indeed, a major thrust of the story is that the risen Christ is the same Jesus the disciples had known before. He is no mere hallucination or vision, but a substantial enough character that he can cook breakfast, and according to Luke's Gospel, even down a bite or two himself.[1] Indeed, the Gospel of John was written in part to debunk the notion, prevalent then and prevalent still, that while Jesus of Nazareth was as dead as the proverbial doornail, the spirit of his teachings lived on without him.

Having tasted the Bread of Life, the disciples warming themselves by the fire that day would never settle for such half-baked pablum. On the beach that day they discovered that the Jesus they so loved and adored was no fallen hero but a living Lord. For while they were awed and unnerved by this encounter with the risen Christ, the text says, "None of them dared ask, 'Who are you?' for they knew it was the Lord." To be sure, he had been marvelously transformed. Yet he was none other than the same beloved Master with whom they'd broken bread a thousand times before.

It is commonly said that religion is a personal matter. But of no faith is that so profoundly true as it is of the Christian faith. For finally, it is not a faith in a body of teaching, however exalted, nor faith in the example of an exemplary life lived long ago. First and foremost it is faith in a person, the risen Lord Jesus, in and through whom God's eternal grace took shape within time.

Will Willimon of Duke Divinity School has taken issue with the impersonal piety often strutted out for civic occasions. At one time he tried to craft prayers for public functions so vague and general in character that they had the capacity to offend absolutely no one. Of course, such formless prayers had no capacity to *move* anyone, either. Finally, after a particularly insipid prayer addressed to "that Divine Force which touches

---

[1] Cf. Luke 24:36-43.

our lives," a student commented to Willimon that such prayers sounded more like those offered by a member of the starship *Enterprise* than a Christian minister. That got Willimon's attention, and from then on he told those seeking his services that he would pray at public functions only as a Christian or not at all.[2]

Generic religion has the same problem as generic cola: it tastes a bit like "the real thing" but lacks the punch of Coca-Cola. Even so, Christian prayer is not addressed to God in general, but to the God and Father of our Lord Jesus Christ. "Jesus" is the "name that is above every name," for Christians dare to believe that the strange power of grace at work in our world is not the trademark of a generic God, but the telltale sign of our risen Lord. Wherever such grace is found, we know he is present as surely as the scent of roses means the buds must be near.

Christian faith is a profoundly personal matter because it is focused in a person, Jesus Christ. And from the other side of the equation, Jesus also considers our relationship to him a very personal matter. The question put to Simon Peter was not, "Simon, do you love the Bible?" or "Simon, do you love my teaching?" or "Simon, do you love my truth?" but "Simon, son of John, *do you love me*?"

The third time Jesus asked that question, it cut Peter to the quick, for it called to mind Peter's threefold denial of his Lord only days before. Plunged into despair by the depth of his betrayal, Simon cried out in anguish, "Lord, you know my heart. You *know* that I love you." And so he did. Jesus graciously restored Peter to his service with the gentle admonition, "Then feed my sheep, Simon; feed my sheep."

Some years ago an executive on the rise at IBM was put in charge of the company's efforts to enter the photocopier market. Those efforts were singularly unsuccessful and resulted in sizable financial losses. Eventually the young executive received the dreaded summons to the office of Mr. Tom Watson, the company president. As Watson talked to the man about the fiasco, the employee's rising anxiety became more and more apparent.

---

2 William Willimon, "When Prayer Goes Public," *Christian Century*, April 15, 1992, 389.

Finally, Watson said to him, "What's wrong, man? You're not hearing me."

After a moment's hesitation, the young executive answered, "Well, it's obvious you're going to fire me."

"Fire you?" Watson exploded. "I just contributed $11 million to your enlightenment!"[3]

In an infinitely greater way, Jesus meets us on the far side of our betrayals, not to scold or dismiss us, but to remind us of the cost of our enlightenment. Having died on the cross rather than renounce either his disciples or his love for them, he comes in the wake of his Easter rising seeking an answering love. He comes to disrupt the petty details and preoccupations with which we while away our lives as he interrupted a failed fishing expedition long ago. And from the distant shoreline of memory to which we have consigned him, he reaches out and taps us with his grace.

We are seized by the awareness of an unseen presence. Then suddenly the eyes of faith open wide: "It is the Lord!" we cry. And there stands Jesus before us reaching to put his hand on our shoulder. Peering deep into our souls, he asks the intensely personal question, "Mary, Sam, Brenda, Paul . . . do you love me?"

Somewhat defensively, we answer, "Lord, I'm an active member of the church. I do my share, give what I can. You know I love you."

"No, no, forget all that," Jesus answers. "I didn't ask you if you loved the church. I want to know *do you love me*?"

We search our hearts for an answer. We remember the time he drew near when we felt forsaken by everyone else. We remember when his grace brought healing to some deep wound of our spirit. We remember the cross on which he bore not merely the world's sin, but our own. Finally, the confession wells up within us, "Yes, Lord, I *do* love you. I love you as the midnight craves the dawn. I love you as the eagle loves the wind. As the deer longs for flowing streams, so my soul longs for you."

---

3 *Pulpit Resource*, May 3, 1992, 17.

"Then feed my sheep," answers the Master. "Tell others of the hope that is within you. For there are people who would give anything to know that the face of God is turned toward them in love."

Then as quickly as he came, he is gone, and we are left with the awesome privilege and heady joy of spreading the news, "That mysterious power of grace at work in our world has a name. The love of God has a face. It is the name and face of Jesus Christ."

And lingering at that shoreline where our despair meets his hope, he yet waits to be our Lord and Master.

We are grateful, O holy Christ, that you have
not remained the anonymous stranger on shore,
but have made yourself known to us.
Now may the mystery of your grace fill and renew us.
For we ask it in the name above every name,
even your own.
Amen.

Questions for Reflection

1. Can you remember a time when you were "surprised by grace" and sensed the risen Christ near? What led you to believe the unseen presence was he?
2. Talk of "God" easily becomes hopelessly vague. If the word "God" were banished from your vocabulary, what would be your preferred name for the One Jesus called "Father"?
3. What did Jesus mean by his instruction to Peter, "Feed my sheep"? (see John 10:1-18). And what does that command have to do with the Church today?
4. Compare the behavior of Peter and the beloved disciple in this passage (21:3,7-8). Which of these two most nearly represents your brand of discipleship?
5. Drawing on your study of John's Gospel—and your own experience—what is required for one to encounter the living Christ today?

A Parting Word

Marilyn Helleberg has written about a time when as a teenager she faced troubling doubts about her faith. One afternoon while doing dishes with her Aunt Alta, the two of them began talking about Easter. Eventually the girl blurted out the question nagging at her: "How can we really know Jesus was raised from the dead? Just because the Bible says it doesn't make it so!"

Her aunt, a farmer's wife, dried her hands on a flour-sack apron: "Come with me, child," she said. Then she led Marilyn across the backyard to a clump of stark, gray bushes the girl took for dead. An icy March wind whipped the branches back and forth as Aunt Alta reached down and cut off some eighteen-inch lengths. They then returned to the house, and the older woman filled a milk-glass vase with water. She put the branches in the vase and set it in the west window in the parlor. Marilyn would later write that the "bouquet of dead branches looked like a bunch of bony-fingered skeletons there, stark and bare."[1]

But in three days those barren branches blossomed into a bouquet of bright yellow flowers, even though the bushes outside were still gray and desolate. Her aunt then explained that just as forsythia bloomed when brought into the house, so Marilyn needed to bring Christ into the living room of her life. Only then could she know firsthand the reality of his resurrection, because his living presence would blossom and flower within her.

It is not enough to read this book—or even John's Gospel—and then wait in detachment for some kind of magic to happen. To encounter the living Christ for yourself, you have to reach

---

1 Marilyn Morgan Helleberg, *God's Best for You* (New York: Macmillan, 1987), 105-7.

out to him in faith and longing. You have to go to the place of your deepest secret and darkest shame and ask him to meet you there. You have to forego your all-wise, all-knowing, self-sufficient routine and ask him to fill you with God's life and love. You have to bring the forsythia out of the yard and into the living room.

In the Book of Revelation the living Christ sounds the cry, "Listen! I am standing at the door, knocking; if you hear my voice and open the door, I will come in to you" (3:20).

Why not take a chance on Jesus and open that door? Invite him in out of the wintry cold cynicism where you have sought to contain him. Ask the Lord of life and love to step off the pages of John's Gospel and into your heart. Do that, *dare* that, and the wonder of Christ's living presence will begin to blossom in you.